DEBILITATING DEMOCRACY

Power From The People

JOSEPH RANDOLPH

Wasteland Press
Shelbyville, KY USA
www.wastelandpress.net

Debilitating Democracy:
Power From The People
by Joseph Randolph

First Printing—February 2010
ISBN: 978-1-60047-408-8

This is a work of fiction. Names, personages, places and incidents other than those referring to Karl Marx are the product of the author's imagination or are used fictitiously. Any resemblance to any actual persons living or dead, excepting Marx, and one incidental reference to President Thomas Jefferson, is purely coincidental. Furthermore, if this fictional tale were actual and true, the story would be frightful and thus possess none of the entertainment value of fiction.

Printed in the U.S.A.

There is a point in the history of a society when it becomes so pathologically soft and tender that among other things it sides even with those who harm it, criminals, and does this quite seriously and honestly. Punishing somehow seems unfair to it, and it is certain that imagining 'punishment' and 'being supposed to punish' hurts it, arouses fear in it. 'Is it not enough to render him undangerous? Why still punish? Punishing itself is terrible.' With this question, herd morality, the morality of timidity, draws its ultimate consequence.

—Frederick Nietzsche

For many will come in my Name, saying, 'I am the Christ,' and will deceive many.

—Jesus

Table of Contents

Letters

To the Reader,

In the most recent election, I was fortunate and favored to receive the powerful advice of a mentor whose brilliance in structuring my campaign assured my political victory. I owe to him an unpayable debt of gratitude. After the unspeakable satisfactions of a year of political fantasy lived out each day in my new political post, I began to contemplate ways to extend the benefits of my mentor's sagely wisdom to others and hopefully in time for the next election. There were two obstacles, however, that until now have delayed the sharing of my teacher's political advisements. One was my frank but selfish fear of embarrassment over my own political naiveté reflected in some of his advice to me. This of course was my own perverse pride that frowned at the thought of my previous political ignorance on exhibition to the world. The other was fear that my mentor's humbleness might prevent him from entertaining my suggestion that his political wisdom might benefit an audience far beyond me. Even more than this, however, I feared that any subsequent fame or notoriety coming to him from publication of his letters might turn his very private life into an unwanted public frenzy. Happily, my mentor, who cares more for the truth than his own leisure, has brushed aside any possible self-interest that might keep his light out of the world. He, unlike me, has been indifferent to his own comforts and foregone any such concerns in his unselfish support for our political cause. That being said, however, I have agreed to his request for him to remain unnamed in this work. As he so profoundly conveyed to me when we settled on this agreement before the publication of the storehouse of his political wisdom, a finite man who has produced something of infinite value should not bury the latter for the fleeting sake of the former.

Ramon Purefoy

Dear Purefoy,

I was very pleased to receive your call. In this day and political climate I must send my consultations by snail mail, as electronic and digital media simply provide unacceptable possibility for interception, and with the matters I will be advising you, we can ill afford anyone looking over our shoulder. In the meantime I will ask you, after study of these advisements, to store them in safekeeping. There is a reelection for you in the future.

Now for the prolegomena. You may fear the venture before you difficult and complex enough to enlist my aid, but the road to political office is an easy venture. This is not to say that it is easy of a kind which anyone on their own could manage, but once having figured this whole political thing out, our work requires no excessive labors. People say knowledge is power, and this, knowledge of politics I mean, is ultimate power. It is like having figured out the laws of nature, with which you may subdue nature herself. We have no such desires regarding Mother Earth, however; the electorate will suffice for us.

What has taken me years to learn, I can distill to you in a few weeks, though it may take more time for you to grasp every detail.

First of all, with our way of thinking we have distinct advantages not shared by our opponents. Having figured out what our opponents have not is of inestimable value against them. Moreover, we have the support of virtually all academics and actors: both the smartest and dumbest in our society. Of course the masses generally suspect the former and have adulation for the latter. That is no great matter, however: the point is that we are not alone, nor outnumbered. What one has to watch is the sheer though lesser number of those who are left. Nevertheless, this number is not so worrisome as it was in the days of the so-called "silent majority." Proponents for that group have largely conceded that their numbers now make them a minority. The most welcome aspect of such a shift in the culture of the country is that without any measures of rank oppression, we are on the brink of a country with virtually only one viable political alternative—ours. This is why among other reasons you have an easy road to travel.

To the uninitiated, I mean unenlightened, it of course does not appear this way, for a variety of reasons. Never mind we have not done so well in the last couple elections. That was only the case simply because we have not distinguished our message from the message of our opponent. And consequently the voters as soon vote for our opponent as for us, and in the coin toss of that, no wonder our luck has been down. A coin toss, however, is not the way to win an election—proven by our rather stale record of late.

So what do you do? There are no insurmountables to worry and fatigue yourself about. You will have the opposite problem of boredom. You have no need to come up with "ideas" with which to lead, for you need not lead, but simply follow the wishes of the people in order to lead. That is, walk out in front of them. Never mind being called a servant, because voters are more than ready to vote for us, once they see that our promises to them are bountiful. Given the weaknesses of human nature, the promises are irresistible. We simply drop the desired goodies in front of the voter, and the voter comes to us. Where we lead they will follow. Though you are a "servant" of the people, people can be made to do just about anything and vote for just about anybody.

Old style politics really did have some substance; we have matter for substance with bushels of symbolism thrown in the mix here and there. I will have more to say about this in forthcoming correspondence.

Dear Purefoy,

What I meant about the symbolism thing is simply this: one of our states has as its motto the words *Esse quam videri*—"to be rather than to seem." It is just the opposite. The father of one of our best understood the difference when he groomed his offspring to see that what is important is not what you are, but what people think you are. I concede that this makes life a bit more complicated—I mean the living of two lives so to speak—but the payoff is huge for us and the money—votes I mean—is virtually immediate. Moreover, even that complication of a double life can be negotiated, as one of our own explained when his private actions gave him public trouble. He persuaded most everyone that infidelity to one need not mean infidelity to another, and better, it need not matter to any, except those to whom it does.

Of course we have some substance, for we are materialists through and through, and nothing could be more substantive than matter. Just ask anyone on the street what is real, and without hesitation they will latch onto something made out of matter. This is an immediate connect with the voter, who is worried about food on the table, a shirt on his back, and a roof over his head. But more about this later.

We believe among other things that politics is ultimate, and that everything is political. This means that we politicize everything, and in terms of getting votes, this works to our advantage. It gives the voter the view that there is nothing that cannot be addressed by political action; he therefore becomes politically active because of it. If there is a tsunami there is a political reason for it; if a bridge collapses there is a political reason for it; if there is a drip at the Arctic there is a political reason for it. If anything out of the ordinary occurs, or for that matter anything ordinary—indeed whatever occurs—there is a political origin somewhere. You see even nature and the workings of nature are not without use for us. We are the ultimate anthropomorphizers, and yet we fault our opponent with having that villainous religious idea of "subduing nature." Our own politicians quit subduing our fragile Mother decades ago; now we are subduing our human political opponents.

Politics is words; I mean it is about the right words, but having recognized this, one cannot take the notion so far as to parse the meaning of the word to fantastic length, for example, as one of our own did some years ago, though with a familiar and common verb. That sort of thing—I mean stretching beyond the limit—is too much even for the mindless public we have these days, even if it is ever so small a word, so there are limits to most anything. This is why we always want to advertise and present ourselves as moderates, and never as extremists—that label we save for introducing and designating our opponents to their unlikely voters. But up to that very distant fence of sounding extreme, one can do just about anything in politics and not just get by with it, but be counted profound or a hero for it. To the tawdry public we come across as having the ability to think outside the box as they call it, and we are held in awe for it. Meanwhile, we put our admirers under and inside our political cage from which there is negligible chance of escape, though our voters think we have liberated them. They are too blind to see we have maneuvered them for our purposes. They, after all, are for us; we tell them, however, we are for them. Words, the right words, I say.

Dear Purefoy,

Oh yes, the coarsening of politics. It comes with tumult of the kind we are attempting in this country. Please refrain from your naive revulsion at it. Just abide by my previous letter. Of course politics is coarsening, but you can lay all the blame on opponents. There is nothing as powerful as taking the argument of your enemy against you and charging him with the fault he lodges against you. More of that later. I see that I must first give you some more milk before you are ready for any meat.

We advance our cause from underneath. That is, we topple, and the way we topple is to convince those watching, or those whose attention we can enlist by proper wordsmithing, that the things that are low in the world—our potential voters—have been made low by the things that are high. This is how we can bring the house down: indeed turn the country on its head. But so as to escape the appearance of negativity, we cloak our demolition in pious high-sounding phrases, like "Social Justice." By it, for example, we can enlist the vote of virtually every housing tenant or renter. And what do we care if we lose the vote of every landlord—mathematically they are of no interest to us; they are always the fewer number. Thus, we are not for the "little guy," but the more guys. I hope you will catch on to how to play this game. We are not for the one, but the ninety and nine.

No, I don't mean you must be a hypocrite; what I meant was that appearance is more important than reality—something I see I must remind you of again. Furthermore, reality is what we make it appear to be. You have to create a reality that people truly want, such that the people, the voters again, want you. This is the sliding down the sliding board part of our job. Think of it this way. We are in effect trying to unteach the population what whole previous generations learned—some time ago now—at their mother's knee. Remember how hard that was for us! No wonder we can shed our adulthood so easily when childhood is offered to us again. Growing up proved painful as we had to pull away from a world we imagined as made for us, a world all about us, and exchange it for the real world, which we then had to strenuously adapt to. But now, with the reeducation we have introduced, and the political platforms we advance, we give all of that previously vanquished world back, and the more we can give back, the more the people give—votes again—to us. How do we do it? Sliding board. Simply persuade the people that the thing standing between them and what they want is not a thing—not inanimate undiscerning matter—but our political opponent. And if they will just push him out of the way they can be home free and done with an opponent who has kept them away. Never blame the voters for anything. Help them find, no, give them a scapegoat—and politicians of our persuasion always have one—our political enemies.

No, no one need ever suffer. When they do, coax them to find someone else to fault for their suffering. Some of our most savvy gurus have coined a few helpful phrases over their tenures in this regard. The one that springs to mind instantly is the nugget that it takes a village to do something you can't do alone. The idea here is one that people can immediately and easily grasp. I mean you cannot go to the moon alone, you cannot run a nuclear facility alone, and so one. You see, people of our persuasion hate the alone thing. We hate people driving in cars alone, or being on aircraft or boats alone. The words public and private in this context are therefore necessary for you and your campaign to master and use. In our eyes everything "private" is of the devil; everything "public" is quartered off and subsumed by government nannies as ready for duty as uncomplaining angels on call for all eternity. Government, of course, governs the public, which is as we want it to be, because we will be in charge of government.

One trick is to get the voter to believe that every failure is because our sense of "community" is insufficiently strong, and that is why we missed success. You weave people so tightly together that you no longer hold them responsible as individuals anymore, because we have erased well nigh all boundaries amongst them. You may need to pull the old "myth of me" trick on occasion because of it. You see, we're not for the individual anymore, though there was a time when we were his greatest champion. No, now we're for the group, or to dress it up with respectability: the common good. Anything less we condemn as just rank selfishness. Thus, what we really want to encourage is the herd mentality or "community." To do this most effectively one must incapacitate individuals until they have no choice but to follow the group, because you've taken everything that was once theirs and given it to the group. That we call community. Our political enemies would kill for all the clout that goes with our vocabulary. Use it often.

Oh, they will howl.

You don't talk to the voters about sacrifice; you talk about satisfactions and those denied them by their enemy. Your voter must think of you as blazing the way in front of them, "fighting for you," we call it. You might remember at the eulogy of one of our late best, some of the mourners got into the act, which is the political act, though they overdid it a bit. At the event there was all kind of oratory about "fighting," and more "fighting," and calling on even our political opponents to "fight," and so on and so forth for the people. You see this is our war and our charge: trying to keep the wolf from the door of the people, and persuading voters that he is nearly in, or will be, except for us. Furthermore, let them know that their wolf is your and their opponent, not those misunderstood woodland varmints that would hurt no one.

With the increasing number of pacifists among us, some are apt to wonder if we have strength sufficient to defend against the enemy without. It is simple—our strength is now directed in full force against the enemy within, for we need not have any enemies without. Here we may be as absolutely vicious on our enemies as the public will allow, remembering the caution I urged earlier. The public won't mind your display of affection for them when you persuade increasing numbers of people that you are fighting public enemy number one for them—your opponent. Remember, you are prepared to be a martyr for them, and to prepare the battleground you must first persuade them that without you they are lost. Drain therefore any energy or devotion they may have directed elsewhere down onto you.

Remember, and if you never knew, it is time to learn it now: persuade the voter that there is nothing between him and his every want, and if there is, get it out of his way. I mean you have to instill in the mind of the voter that you can safeguard him from all sorts of vicissitudes and traumas and tragedies that stifle his aspirations. If this all starts to smell of religion, then you have an inkling of the idea. Moreover, if your voter is religious, you need to instruct him to see his religious allegiances under his political allegiances and not the reverse. If he is still living under some archaic notion of things belonging to God that don't belong to Caesar, convince him, and you must—but prudently do it in a private meeting—that there is no God. Ours is a still a religious country after all, so exercise caution. If you cannot tilt him all the way in our direction, try convincing him that his God wants him to give his money to Caesar, even if God has to take a cut or maybe get nothing. In a country such as ours that may take some doing, but the day will come. If we persist we can oust the old God with a kind of political force to match some of our foreign models.

Dear Purefoy,

Your last letter reveals that I must go back to pre-prolegomena for you. No, the only thing that matters is how well you can persuade voters that their government is prepared to give them everything the government has until it cannot give anymore. Even then, you must persuade the people that the government is still prepared to give. We as politicians need not lead, but simply follow the wishes of the people in order to lead. By so doing, we convey to our voters that there are onerous objects between themselves and their desires, mammoth obstacles, and only the work of government can remove them. Without telling them so directly, convey to them that without us, they can do nothing. To put it positively, talk about "building community." It has a familiar ring, and remember you are a "servant" of the people, and when the people catch onto that—that they have a servant whose only required payment is their vote—you will be in their employ forever. Wherever they lead we will follow—that, my boy, is democracy in action, except as I said in an earlier correspondence, we are aware of who is leading. We can simply use such high sounding phrases as "will of the people," and citizens will grovel before those of us prepared to serve the will of the people. Of course we have to prepare the people for their will. This we do by persuading them that they may have as they wish. Remember what I said: we are reeducating adults to be children.

This is one reason we make so much of children, because we present ourselves as their protectors against all that may harm them. We are essentially trying to make adults like them, and one thing needed to make that work is to render these adults as little children who come to us with their arms extended.

This should not be above your understanding. Look what our associates have accomplished for us to date and how we can use it all for our advantage. Examples are everywhere. We have, as you know, been called the bleeding hearts. Well, there was a time when no man with a plan for power dared even show the natural moisture around his eyes; now, however, he can cry his face wet and empower his base because he did it. You see, it is the thing about children again. No one expects them at their young age to take on the world without a tear, so now, so too us. The thing we were previously disparaged for is now expected, indeed demanded of us.

We are the party that is "for the children." Do not forget that phrase and use it frequently. You see the trick is to get behind a phrase that everybody is afraid to shoot at and you shall have unfailing protection, like a bulletproof vest. It is rather like the force of the Mafia if you think about it, and we need not even resort to violence.

Dear Purefoy,

Your last letter reveals that I must go back, again, to pre-prolegomena for you. No, the only thing that matters is how well you can persuade voters that their government is like Santa Claus.

Who says you cannot legislate morality? We are in the morality business, but of a certain kind. We don't presume to trespass on personal territory by passing out any list of do's and don'ts—that is the burden our opponent carries—to our immense advantage. We call his effort to shackle us to his Ten Commandments suppression of liberty and so forth. We, however, are the true moral party because we are prepared to take money from people to give it to those without. The whole compassion thing as we intend it is built around the ethic of what is yours is mine—made into law.

Persuade the voter that money is not the object when money is the object. Most people don't care whether the country goes broke as long as they remain solvent. Therefore, they care little for talk about "balancing the nation's budget" and more about how you will contribute to theirs.

Ideas are for people who want to and can think, but keep any ideas discussion distant from your voters. We have so few idea people in our targeted electorate that appealing to them considered as a block of voters is mistaken because it is a stupid statistical mistake. Remember, we live in a democracy, not an academy. That being said, we have the best of both worlds, because we now, and have for some time, controlled much of both.

Of course the government doesn't have any money. It only distributes what it prints or takes from the people. So what? People don't care where their money comes from anymore than they care about the morals of the leaders who lead them. A dollar given is a dollar whether it came from a saint or a scoundrel, so after a while you concern yourself only with the money. If someone offers you money, do you ask about the repercussions to the giver? Of course not!! We simply lend the impression, already strong in society and getting stronger by the hour, that government is a source of eternal money that will never run dry. Of course some people, though they are soon to be extinct, do not think this is the "role" of government, but we have an arsenal of ammunition against them. If some opponent dares to be so foolish as to point out that the "cost" of so and so program will bankrupt the country, ask him if people or money is more important, and if you are in a public setting—where you can derive maximum voter benefit in such an exchange—this reply will be sufficient to make him look a devil who delights in watching people writhe in misery to the point of death. But at this point your work will be over, for the crowd will do the rest to him. And take a trip down the sliding board again. Meanwhile, you have portrayed yourself as a saint who cares more for people than money.

Dear Purefoy,

Yes, of course we are trying to be more like our neighbors across the Atlantic, but we do not say so in as many words. To do so can court real disaster. One of our own slipped some time ago in lauding them as "so far ahead of us," and a savvy opponent asked if he meant the secularism or socialism. Of course our speaker meant both, but could not stand behind the word of either.

Of course, we are more prosperous than our Atlantic neighbors, but remember, we do not get ourselves elected by pointing to our successes, but by attesting to their lack. We must create work for ourselves, though not because of our failures as a consequence of our political point of view, but our failures as a country, and then we rack up all of them as the responsibility of our opponent's point of view. We don't have to do this alone. Fortunately, we even have movie makers helping us with this enterprise these days, showing, for example, the deplorable state of how we attend to our sick, compared to the natural mothering instincts of our neighbors across the Atlantic, and even some neighbors to the south of us. Our country, by contrast, is brutal.

You want to portray our country as unfinished, in fact hugely unfinished, and indeed so much so that we, from our point of view, see the necessity of constructing a new country. You see if we applaud and laud successes, people have the notion that things are looking up, so we have to and must point out any and all gaps, cracks, crevices, crashes, and catastrophes as demanding our attention. We do not therefore congratulate ourselves inordinately, because the voter yearns to hear what more we can give him, rather than what you just gave him. That he already has. This is why we are such busybodies, while avoiding that appearance. Remember, again, that all things are, or can be made, political; therefore, until utopia comes, we will be in business.

Dear Purefoy,

You must belong to our opponents. Did someone give you my name by accident? Are you a spy? We don't want "intelligent voters." We simply want voters. The adjective only matters if it is a number, and preferably a large one and not of course a name, because the vote of anyone is equal to the vote of anyone else. We do want voters to be as herdable as possible, and heaven knows we have supported an educational system that has made supernatural gains in the loss of even ordinary knowledge. Do not underestimate the raw power of voter ignorance, especially when it comes with great numbers. The inquisitive voter you want to avoid, but you will not have to avoid many because there are not many to avoid. And you can turn their attack on you against them. As example, our opponent has a huge burden to bear these days, for he lacks something that we all tout: "compassion." Living in dread of the charge of not being "compassionate," their party tries to look "compassionate," and their candidates will feebly try to look the part, holding and kissing babies—all the usual stuff. But we need not worry, for their every effort is in vain, for we have sufficient and satisfied voters on our side to make any such claims look like an attempt to play catch up. If your opponent is using your slogans and your language you can be assured he is losing in his mind. Some of our opponents have capitulated to this folly by trying to out-give us, for example, in terms of the money we promise voters. Truth is, they can't do it, and they know it, because they painfully know we are prepared to give it all. Why they persist under this delusion, we do not know. What we do know is that they are doomed when they try.

Yes, I know that the posture of the opposition puts them at a great disadvantage. They apparently have no spine and appear at times to believe even less in their principles than we in ours. They are terrified of being branded as without compassion, the party of the rich, disdainful of the poor and so on. Their fear of such labels is so great they exert massive energies in their desperation to prevent the feared impression. It is amazing to me that they only rarely try on us what we do to them. They never pin our tail on us. One wonders whether they lack a spine or a brain or both.

I will admit at times I have wished for a stronger opponent, one that would give us something of a fight at least once in a while for sheer fun. They are, however, I am content to say, adequate for our purposes, wanting though they be.

If you must know, yes, we have some ideas. "Ideology," we call it. I suspect you want more than this, however. What I think you want is for me to tell you whether we actually believe in our own ideas, or whether we know the ideas are dubious, but persist with them nonetheless, because they lure voters to us. That they work for us is sufficient. One of the most effective ways for sending votes your way from every direction, though it takes quite a bit of political skill, is to posture yourself toward the potential voter in one way, but position yourself toward another potential voter another way. This way one can maximize the number of voters listening and ultimately voting for you.

Whether we believe in our ideas or not is beside the fact, because the fact is that they work!! If you would promise each voter, that upon your election, you will place $3,000.00 in their bank account, or create an account for them to put it in, you could go to sleep on election night and not rest on mere dreams of winning the next day, but the reality. In fact, one of our own tried something like this, though with a much larger sum. You see our world is a world where dreams and reality are one, because we will tell voters we will make the reality fit their dream. That is why I told you in my very first letter, that there is virtually nothing to do when you run for office with us. Perhaps attack your opponent a bit, if he is particularly feisty, but your larger problem will be boredom. You see, instead of that old adage, mistakenly used by some of our own, that we should ask what we can do for our country, we teach the people that there is no end to what the country can provide for them. Man, we are on a gold mine, and it is us and our message. No opponent preaching "responsibility" or any other stodgy word has a chance against us. This is why we have every justification for saying we have a "new" message.

Dear Purefoy,

Of course the press is on our side! Why do you think our rich opponents have to and do raise so much more money than we; simply because we have a huge campaign waged for us by the media and for not a nickel from us. You see that is why we were so energetic a short time ago to reform the laws on campaign contributions. If we can tighten the noose around these contributors to our opponents we will strangle both, meanwhile our campaign goes on unabated, unchecked in the compliant obedient press which plugs our cause without fail. Without them, we would be worse off than we have been in recent elections.

I presume you watch the networks where the "side" they are on is not just apparent, but neatly blatant. Of course they provide some token criticism of our candidates on occasion, but it is rare occasion. The presses are masters of persuasion because they are masters of pessimism. They are always raising "questions," of course grounded in that most helpful of democratic doctrines: the right of the people to know. You can make the free press notion of our country work with our political notions about everything.

However, and thank goodness, the press in fact decides what the people will be told and what the people will therefore know. God help us the day the people take the press in their own hands. The people know what they are told to know. Most citizens never imagine that the media might have a side on the issues they spin, or that they leave out a bit of the news they find inimical to their political proclivities. That is why the so-called independent presses and talk-radio are our thorns in the flesh. They tell different stories. You see, our press, though not by any means run without brains, is living in a bygone era by persisting in the archaic belief that they are objective with regard to their reporting of the news. There is no such thing!! At least some of the other press admits it, and I suspect in time so will our willing minions in the press be forced into admitting it too. But that day is far away and probably not even during your young lifetime. Meanwhile, you have an election to win.

Dear Purefoy,

You ask for examples of how the press pads our party. Do you watch your television, or more likely given your apparent ignorance, I would ask if you own one? If not, go to a store, where they have them on broadcasts for potential buyers to watch. You need to have your eyes checked after a glance or two at the screen, unless your hearing is also wanting. There are not enough trees or paper in this town for me to give you all the examples, but I will give some, since apparently you are unable to see—yes, I said see, not detect, not deduce, since it is present for either the eye or the ear.

Some time ago one of the media ran a story about the fear of AIDS transmission among the population and entitled it "A Disease Called Fear." This cast it, of course, in the unfounded fear category, as the story constituted a rebuttal of unwarranted fears concerning transmission of the virus. Now suppose they had run a story by the same name, with the subject, however, being fear of second hand smoke. This is a sound fear, a fear we are supposed to have. So, you see, our press gets to decide what is to be feared and not feared. What more could you ask for? They no more report "just the news," than I just order what I order from the restaurant menu.

Another example comes to mind. I remember one of ours interviewing a group of silent majority gurus some years ago, before their numbers started to slide and then plummet. Before our reporter was through with them, they looked like ignoramuses. They were lamenting how the country had degenerated and so on and on without end. Finally the interviewer innocently asked what "form" this degeneration had taken, while his facial expression and voice tone provided the real rope for lynching them. When he asked his question it was done with facial contortions befitting asking a bunch of people claiming to have been kidnapped by aliens, the day and time they had been taken captive. You see the trick is to shade and tilt the interview by the words and intonation of your question. By such tactics, one can intimate that there is nothing wrong at all.

Have you not heard our political opponents decry the fact that we have the press in our hands? I fear you have been apolitical, and this is not a trait that will contribute to your success as a candidate of our political persuasion. That aside, the moaning of our opponents is constant about this press relationship we have, so of late, as I said earlier, they have created some of their own news outlets. Still, however, we never admit our relationship, only criticize theirs. And as I said, I suppose the time will come when our press will have to admit their perspective is our perspective, but until they do, we can go on doing what we are doing until we are sent a bill.

Dear Purefoy,

Of course we tell everybody how bad off they are and who has put them in this predicament. Fear is our noblest weapon. In the old days people were told how far they were from God, so they would flee to God for mercy; we now tell them how bad off they are, so they can flee to government. We care nothing for God, less for religion, but will use the proclivity toward both for our gain when we can. Doctor Marx would not be pleased with us. However, we do no worse than the wretched capitalist who told his workers the more they slaved for him, the more crowns they would have in capitalist heaven.

We, of course, being intelligent people have no dubious heaven to offer, so we offer all the heavenly riches right here on earth, for we are secular materialists through and through. We do not, like the religious, worry as to whether our name is written in the book of life, but whether it is on the government check. That piece of paper is a lot surer than any heaven that keeps out people whose God is money.

When our opponent interjects their brand of religion into their campaign we can stifle it by mention of a few convenient phrases, like Dark Ages or Inquisition or Witch Trials, but of late our best, by way of warning: that the separation of church and state in our country is being compromised. We, of course, have our own men and women of the cloth to preach our message. We never worry about their religious ideas, because they are as committed to earth as we are, and as doubtful of heaven as we. Their heaven is on earth, like ours, so working together presents few problems, for their god is as solvent as ours. Therefore, we can create all kind of religious posturing for our religious voters simply by our associations with these select men and women of the cloth.

No, you do not have to lose your religion to side with us, but you do have to find a new one. As you can see on any clear political day, we have men and women of the cloth with us, and visibly so, and when you listen to them, you know without any doubt that they are one of us and with us. Oh yes, the other side has its holy men too, but they are the type prepared to leave politicians over religious principles. Our clergy have no such choice available; we, and what we stand for, constitutes their religion. Remember the old time religion that said, "Thou shalt have no other gods before me." We still honor that commandment fervently, but not the god who commanded it.

You intimate that we have all the marks of the religious and you are right. The reason is simple. Our political ideas are our religion. That is why we don't want religion in politics, because then we would have a competitor. We don't like, no, more, we loathe competition. That is why we always prefer the public to the private; it is not without reason that we only grudgingly and with much gnashing of teeth, concede the power of the free market to feed and clothe the world. The more we take from the private sphere, the sooner we will have it all.

Of course, our opponents are a different kind of religious, but you can use it against them. Throw one of the volatile words I suggested at them and they will see their poll numbers descend so rapidly that their belief that there is a God will become a matter of doubt to them. Better yet, fasten onto the divisive nature of religion, and portray your opponent as dividing rather than uniting the people. Think of yourself as a pied piper rather than as some sort of Napoleon. Indeed, as the piper the job is much easier. Remember, if going down the sliding board is getting harder, you're doing something wrong.

My word, think of some of our dearest causes, and how they ring with the association of religion to anyone watching. Take as example, our support for the rights of a child. To those with only the briefest acquaintance with the Gospel stories, our effort simply looks like a modern and therefore correct version of Jesus chastising the disciples who would shoo children away from him.

About your other worry. You need not bother about wrongdoing that befalls us on occasion. We have developed a response to that charge that brings no retort. We simply say that we are all sinners, and most of the religious think we must be saints by conceding that we are all sinners. The fact of the matter is that all the sinners are not sinning all the time, but our opposition never realizes that, because they are trying to come down off their holier than thou mountain after their accusation against us is turned against them. We, meanwhile, appear as humble as the dog on the hearth, though we stole dinner.

Dear Purefoy,

Yes, you should refrain from too much inflammatory language, unless the occasion calls for it. On the other hand, there are plenty of occasions meriting such language—and the best thing is the votes it brings. Outrage is indeed one of our best vote-getters, because we are most attractive to the political eye and ear when we are in our fiery prophetic mode; the people, that is, the voters, are spell-bound by the daring accusations we make, and soon, by hearing us make them often enough, they start to make them too because they now believe them, and soon the whole country is doing what we taught them to do. Yes, we are really teachers, and effective ones at that. Anyone who can accomplish what we have done with a voter population that now eats out of his hand is to be rewarded with office.

The way you do it is to appeal to their tawdry side: the complaining side that sees in their every misfortune someone to blame. You see, we really are trying to reeducate adults to be the worst kind of children again.

What I mean is simply that you let people know how little they are in charge of their lives. In other words, there are huge malevolent forces conniving every waking moment to oppress them. One has to be very, very careful here, because what you must do is convince them that if we can only get these horrible people out of the way, and all the maliciousness that goes in their wake, then voters can make and mend their lives as they wish, without anyone noticing that we are still hanging around afterward. Thus, we talk about "institutional" this and that as oppression that lingers, and in effect, never ends. This, of course, requires continuous monitoring, and then our programs never end, nor the need for us, because the oppression never ends. We therefore have guaranteed employment extending into the infinite future.

Yes, our whole program lives off of promoting fear—get used to it, and better yet, like it. And better still: manufacture a few new types to use. It works this way. No matter how good anything and everything is going for anybody and everybody, go and find someone—the compliant press is always good for this—who has lack. Such people are always to be found, because we are a big country. When you find them, however much time and energy it took, cast them as the norm, and not the exception, so that all who hear you imagine that what you are saying is much larger than it is. Then bring the compassion thing in. It works without fail.

Yes, you need to become familiar with and also skillful in using our stock phrases. You know them already because they have become part of our culture because of us, and thus we are the predominant culture. "Where do you draw the line?" Another one is "gray areas." "Compassion" I have already alluded to. For those of religious bent, "Who am I to judge?" Any sin committed, to use the religious jargon, is nullified by the fact that we are all sinners. Thus, to punish the sinner, and to be "just" about it, we must punish ourselves. To avoid that we don't punish the sinner, but only if he is one of ours.

You really can have your cake and eat it with us too. For example, some have asserted that our politics are Christian. Thus, in the same breath, some have dared use the words Christian socialism together. Not of course in this country, except at the very local level. Of course this makes some of our own nervous, until they notice that where the two have blended, the country in time is largely left with only one, for religion simply goes by the wayside and eventually shuffles away. Oh what a world we live in. One would almost think it had been made for us. Maybe there is a God.

Dear Purefoy,

You ask where we are going as a party. You need to cleanse your soul of what is eating at it. We are going to . . . be elected! Elected for the sake of being elected. Of course we don't say this to the electorate. There we call ourselves public "servants" along with other high-sounding verbiage. That being said, even I will admit that it completely stymies me how the public can think of any of us as servants. Tell me, what servants do you know who make more than their "masters?" On the other hand, if the discrepancy is noticed we simply point out that unless we continue to garner exorbitant wages, no public servant will desire to serve anymore. You see there is a posturing answer for any and every question, no matter how damaging the inquiry may look in the beginning.

So you are still brooding over my assertion that the press is in bed with us? And you asked what happened to a "free" press. They're still free, just freely associating with us. They are scarcely any better, at least most of them, at separating their opinion from a fact than any of us. If you doubt this, do some research.

Ah, the military. It serves as one of our best political weapons. We are constantly telling voters how much more we could be giving them if we did not give to the killing machines we call the military. Rarely will one ever ask you what the function of the military is, because we have indoctrinated the voter with the belief that the spigot of government money is for him, and he cannot imagine it being for anything else. Being diverted away from him to kill people when none want to see people killed makes no sense—he instead wants the spigot going full throttle again for him.

If we want people killed because they are trying to kill us, of course that is a weighty problem. And once in a while a dastardly enemy shows up who hates us, and we have to rattle the saber a bit to scare them away. Some of them will go away, or you can put them off long enough, that, heaven forbid, a person of the opposition gets elected, and he must deal with the problem rather than us. But most problems are not that severe. You might remember that one of our opponents advocated a shield of some sort that would keep enemy projectiles from ripping into our country, but we mocked at it enough that we got the people to believe something more absurd. This was the idea that holding up a shield to our antagonists would provoke them to throw a spear, and therefore if we removed the shield they would throw down their spear.

Naturally, we have a tense relationship with the military. I mean people like us who want to see weapons taken from citizens are not going to love the people holding the remaining ones. We are scarcely ever an advocate for this group except for very particular reasons of prudence and expedience, because they do not ordinarily vote in our direction. I think the only hope we have to draw more of them to our side is to show the futility of the whole war thing. In many ways this should not be hard, and one wonders why we have not been more zealous with our soldiers to show them the futility of what they do.

Finally, we might point out, like a few of our own have suggested, that the choice of the military is really no choice. One has to be very careful here, for we can get caught in trouble with such an insinuation. Words, remember, words; the right ones in the right places doing the right things can work wonders for you—I mean votes.

Dear Purefoy,

Ah yes, patriotism. One must know how to play this card skillfully with the people. We, of course, hate the mere idea because it connotes the parochial mind that thinks their country can never be wrong, simply because they have never seen another country. Furthermore, advocates of patriotism tend to advocate demonization of their enemies. We, by a plan of genius, demonize ourselves, to show that we leave no stone unturned, not even our own. Therefore, we have been so scrupulous with our self-examination that no one else bothers to examine us, for we have already examined ourselves. Socrates would be proud of us until he probed further. You see, we get to police ourselves!! You ask to what advantage? Simply this.

We present ourselves as the party that is so self-scrutinizing because we will not allow ourselves exemption from the same sort of scrutiny with which we judge our enemies.

I will admit that negotiating with an enemy is a bit difficult when he is doggedly resistant, like the empire one of our worst political opponents once imagined. I mean there really are some things we cannot say. Though the leash we allow ourselves is long and in most cases ample for our purposes, it is still a leash with a finite amount of length. Thus one cannot simply say anything wished, for we must maintain at least a smidgen of reality in our contentions. One cannot, for example, maintain that conditions in our country are worse than one where the majority of citizens stood in lines for hours for a few ounces of meat.

But with that difficulty out of the way, we can really go to work on most everything else, and look pointedly at the mammoth sins of our country, and where there chance to be few, invent more. The trick is not complex. Complex and sophisticated people such as we are, we must always portray ourselves as open-minded, by beating ourselves as did that undeserving publican before the righteous Pharisee. No one ever figures that we are really the Pharisee because we do such a good job of portraying our enemy as one.

Yes, you should play our current unpopularity in the world as reason to reject our political opponents. One should never question why we are unpopular; one can simply point out that we are. Rarely will one ask if perhaps there is a good and not bad reason that we are not popular in the world. You see, the impetus, the pressure to go along with the crowd these days is generally sufficient to disallow any position to the contrary of the crowd. Yes, the world is ripe for us because it resembles sheep waiting to bleat approval of what all else say, and if they say it loud enough, the solitary voices voicing any protests will be drowned. We can hardly imagine a better state of affairs, because by sheer shrillness, forget reason, we can win. If you have ever watched a football game in a stadium full of fans, when the home team calls upon those fans to make so much noise that the opponent team cannot even hear the play being called for, then you have the idea. Don't let them be heard, though not by gagging them, but by drowning them in a sea of voices that make them unhearable. Oh, life is good when one has no opponents—or none that can be heard.

Yes, the international community is our ultimate court of appeal because we must project our image as one seeking the good of all, the global good; therefore we must never ever be thought of as loners and not team players. Dialogue is our toy. We toss it around as always preferential to violence and war, with, of course, the contention that anyone for peace could never favor war.

The opposition is always trying to justify the overthrow of despots with force. There is one response to that savagery that will silence such a notion, and it is this: "One does not export democracy down the barrel of a gun." You see how it works, though we have no brief for either. Nevertheless, we can ignore the fact that democracy and guns go together against tyranny. The fact of the matter, moreover, which the opposition never brings up as counter response is that virtually any and every democracy has been birthed with guns, because few dictators are willing to yield to democracy without a fight. You see, despots are so opposed to democracy that the people must take up an armed rebellion to secure any freedom. We, however, want to distance ourselves from violence of any sort by use of dialogue. Remember, peace is our ultimate goal, and not freedom as our opponents would have it. This is why equality and talk of "community" is infused into our conversation all the time.

Dear Purefoy,

Yes, with our opposition the poor tend to get left out; with us they become the centerpiece. The other party slights them for the most part because they never see much of them, nor for very long, and because the other party will desire to educate them out of their poverty. With our opponents, who the poor are is always changing, because our opponents instruct and show them how to escape the plight of poverty. They want the poor to assimilate to themselves. We, however, build some public housing, and tell them to stay for a while. If they spend their life there, it is no worse for us, but the better, because we garner their vote of thanks every election. We never want to release a voter that we catch.

We, contrary to our opponent, know much more about the poor, because we get to see so much of them, and we are thus thoroughly familiar with their plight. And we never let them go, that is, go on to be something else. Once we have them we always have them, and that perpetuates the animosity of the other party, who can never figure out why they favor us. You see, the other party wants them to combat their poverty, and gets them to believe they can. With us, however, the opposite is true.

Of course we go after the rich, and we can afford to, because they are so few. Their vote is no more than any other vote—that is the genius of our democracy. A scoundrel, as long as he is breathing, has a vote worth as much as that of any rich man. And even that is not an absolute requirement, as we have been known to have the dead cast a vote our way when really needed. Ah, we have pursued the leveling tendencies of democracy to the point that there will be little freedom left where we gain ascendency. The other side has pursued freedom so fiercely that it has left much for levelers like us to level.

We of course have to be careful about that rich thing in a time when good shares of the population have decent bank accounts. Of course one need not worry too much, because envy will do for us what we could never do but for it. Human nature is thus on our side. I must give envy the due owed its name: we live by it and on it and through it. One vote lost for castigating the rich will result in fifty more won by castigating the rich. Yes, we are the party of the community, the common good. We are like a mob looking to silence those who don't march with us. Few can withstand our intimidation.

Yes, one does have to be careful here because the whole thing is rather like a balancing act. Everything must work together. Thus, our emphasis on diversity and pluralism has to be emphasized in a way that does not impugn our attempt to wipe it out. The diversity thing came about as a way to knock down the kingpins because they were kings. The whole academic establishment has adopted the heresy as gospel, so too, the media and actors: nearly all are at our beck and call. Therefore be a patron of their work, whether of the screen or the stage or the page.

Yes, you should by all means challenge your opponent to a debate. Talk about him as a thief before your listeners. Sound alarmist with reference to him and his way. Portray him as an extremist. Remember what I told you a while back. Portray him as the reason for your voter's failures. Don't blame the voter; don't even come close to any suggestion of that. Instead, blame your opponent politician, because blaming him gives the voter all kinds of hope by finding fault elsewhere. This gives the voter everything he wants; he's off the hook; you're off the hook with him; you get everything you want; and your opponent gets nothing. Sliding board, all sliding board.

A little more coaching about debate technique is in order. You want to portray your opponent as public enemy number one. No matter what his good record, his achievements, or his integrity, don't let your listener think the candidate has any of those things. Soon your opponent will grow angry at you for doing this, and he will try for audience sympathy by portraying you as some sort of inhuman vicious attack dog. Nothing could be a better set up for you. Let your listeners know that you are an attack dog—for them! Then, despite our hatred of all things violent and military, let loose with a barrage of denunciations against him, because you want the voters to know that you are fighting for them, when fighting him. How followers love that word. Never infer to them that they might fight for themselves.

Yeah, I know. We used to say we are all only a heartbeat from eternity; now we tell them we're all only a paycheck away from starvation. You see, we tout diversity—for our purposes—but have no belief in it, and try to show everybody that we are all alike as the basis of impugning those unlike us. We of course want to proclaim to everybody that everybody is the same, and if they are not, oppression is the inevitable cause and reason for it. We do not want even one "extraordinary" in our sea of the ordinary.

Dear Purefoy,

Yes, I'm afraid it is more or less true what you say. Our contempt for the masses of Americans is evident, but we disguise it behind profundities that send the masses ranting about our brilliance instead of our contempt. We have all sorts of high-sounding phrases to exhibit our worthiness to serve our fellows in whatever capacity we can be of service. You will need to train yourself in such phrases and how to use them. "For the children" never fails, and the best of it is that by implication the ignorant populace infers that our political enemies are against the children. Imagine how impossible their burden is as they try chiseling away from that public perception.

Yes, the "disenfranchised." This one has been around a few years now, and has yielded an untold number of votes for us and without a doubt will continue to produce astronomical numbers. It is part of the poor voter ploy—where we inform the voter, the citizen again, that their troubles are created by someone else creating their trouble. In other words, there are thieves among us, and they have stolen from us. Where there are few or not enough "disenfranchised" we create more, in the same way that we create a world of fabricated suspicion against our political enemy. Thus, we talk about the rich people invested in the stock market, but if anybody would look, they would know just how many citizens are invested.

Oh, profundity. You see people really don't want a leader who thinks like them; no, they want someone who can think above them, ahead of them, someone that they can rely upon to do their thinking for them—that last one we really crave, and we generally are not disappointed with the number allowing us to do their duty. You see, the voters really don't want someone like themselves: they want someone living a step up. Oh yes, we also like to tout our working class, immigrant, rags to riches origins, but that spin is really a lot less effective with voters than the candidate who shows his intellect as superior to others. To show yourself as such is really quite easy. To show the simple our profundity not much energy is required. Sometimes you can simply toss a phrase that is a little on the side of the mundane, and by just the right inflections elevate it to a statement that will be construed as divine utterance.

Dear Purefoy.

No, you fool, you don't have to be overtly hostile to traditional religion. In fact, it is the political kiss of death to show your whole hand on this one. But be that as it may, there is a much more effective ploy, one that totally dispenses with your worry, and it has the opposite effect. We masquerade as closer to God than the God worshippers. There are numerous ways to do it. I have presumed you are of at least normal intelligence, so I can give you a few examples, and thereafter you can come up with a few of your own.

We often take the side opposite our political opponent, and then the opponent charges us with being for the enemy, indeed traitorous, as you must have witnessed for yourself. So we, for example, argue for the prisoners we detain, and argue against ourselves as their detainers. We reach deep, and argue that in so doing we are seeking out the lost sheep, the lost coin, and in this we follow the example given us by the religious. This move flummoxes our opponent. So, another example, already mentioned; we bring up the "we're all sinners" argument, to show how nonjudgmental we are. Indeed, as you know, our opponent's judgments are largely couched in their religious beliefs; we have none, nor do we want any, so our nonjudgments flow simply from our likes and dislikes, as arbitrary or as positivist as you like them. But to our dear voters, it looks like we are truly the party of the religious. So there you have it—again—we can have our cake and eat it too.

Of course we are concerned about the environment and desperately so. That is, it is the conduit through which we give ourselves metaphysical importance, because we have shredded every bit of it in high places. It is our new anthropomorphism. All those religious types used to imagine the universe was made for them by their God, and that their cosmic importance derived from this fact. We all know there is no such fact these days; there is just us, and that by default. In other words, we're in charge of ourselves, because nothing else is. That would be too tough a pill for our poor and ignorant citizen, much less our religious voters to swallow, so to satisfy our unanswered hunger we do give ourselves cosmic importance—but it's simply in the damage we know we can do to our dearly beloved Mother Earth. I mean that is what gives us what standing we have—we can ruin the world. Of course the ruiners are our opponents, not us. I call it thus the new anthropomorphism, but of course it is in reverse. And frankly for us who know better, it's not much of a consolation, but for the voters it will work, and for us it will have to do.

Dear Purefoy,

No, you fool, we adore money as much as anybody. But we cannot let money appear to control us; we must manage it ever so carefully. To our voters we must have every appearance of loathing money, and meanwhile punctuate our loathing with the remorseless implication that a man making money must love money more than people.

The fact of the matter is that we need more money than is to be had in all the world, for with the mammoth kind of government we envision we require a bottomless well of it. Putting this loving and loathing of money together is an art form we have perfected and few of the public ever penetrate the mystery of how you can loathe money and always be ready with cash in hand for their hand. Meanwhile we have our cake and eat it too, or, have our money and hate it too. We take from the few and give to the many. People concerned with making money, and in particular those who make lots of it we despise, but we use them and their hated money to stoke the hatred of the masses for them and their monstrous amount of money. Meanwhile, the masses that constitute way more people—the statistic is overwhelming—are the ones we appeal to in their hatred of the moneyed minority. You see we claim to be about equality, but we classify and demonize as we conquer. We love the us and them discrimination and use evocative language like the "digital divide" to evoke sympathy for the less fortunate. On the other hand, you can have recourse to the ageless admission of the barbaric inequalities between the haves and have-nots. Everybody knows what you mean, and better, they think what we have taught them to think; the have-not's are where they are because of the haves.

Of course we need the hated ones, for they provide our money. We treat them like we treat cigarettes; we hate them in public, and count the taxes they generate for us in the back room like children swooned on Christmas morning.

One does need to exercise a little caution, at least for now, but in a few more years, perhaps in a decade or so, we can come right out and use the word that our every action portends. I mean, of course, that now we can only use it privately but never publicly, until some time to come: the word—socialism. As an elected official you can help with this by using the term free-market and capitalism interchangeably, for we want the easy opprobrium into which the word capitalism connotes greed to spill over negatively into the association of freedom with someone's greed producing someone else's poverty. You see freedom is the springboard of difference, and differences breed inequalities, which we are supposed to hate, and diversity, which we purport to love, we also hate. But we need it, because this a balancing act, that is, keeping the cash cow producing while we practically disembowel her every April 15th and at the cash register year round. This requires carefully chosen words in public. On the other hand, the widening gap between rich and poor, which we lament to the skies, we never wish to see cease, for then you and I shall cease as viable candidates for the people's votes. Remember the words of our 19th century architect. If our plan succeeds, government will wither away—that my boy would be a disaster for us: we who have our being in, with, and through it. Remember too his other words, the beginning of our political shenanigans—that all history is the warfare between classes. Therefore, it must never come to an end; when it does we shall end; for there shall be no need for us.

Dear Purefoy,

Divide and conquer is good political advice and better yet a sumptuous recipe for election. You see, you have a single opponent, but his voters by and large share two minds; divide them and you can vanquish or at least cripple both. Thus, we need a battle plan against both.

One group of our opponents praises liberty as if it were God; for we who believe in neither, we speak of the atrocities of liberty, the "free" market and its ultimate savage conclusions. We can also call that market "godless" when among religious ears, for they will especially appreciate the connation, and perhaps start to doubt that we are so irreverent and immoral after all. The really radical libertarians, who we are also working against, are nevertheless like us in one way here, for they believe in absolute autonomy of the individual. The autonomy, however, is for we who rule.

For all our venom against aristocracy and monarchs we live like them and see ourselves as such. These libertarians, however, prefer a society with next to no government, and loathe any government that dares to dictate or frankly suggest any higher or moral life its citizens should take up because the government thinks so. Thus unlike us, they really, for the most part, would scarcely mind no government at all, which, as I said before, would be our doom.

The other group within our opponents constitutes another kind of problem, and I think a more difficult one. This group thinks the government is supposed to restrain evil, and so on and theological so forth. This group tends to be more religious and rankly so. Herein lies the difficulty.

What they call good we call evil and what they call evil we call good. Don't think, however, that this is a completely formidable problem. The trick, which I suggested some time ago is this: out-religion them. You know what I mean. Use their Own against them; twist his words to make them ours; after a while they will cease to read his words, because they have Ours. And in so doing they will think they have him.

So what started for you as an insuperable conundrum ends up as child's play. Just remember, however, that they want to be coddled by their God, but we want to coddle them and throw their god out. Remember, we do not like competition, because if it is our judge long enough, we will fail. If, however, we can do well enough in that competition, they will forget the flames of their hell while living in the dollhouse we have made for them, and we will have succeeded in subjugating a minority class of slaves, the wealthy in other words, to provide it all for them.

Dear Purefoy,

Oh yes, education. It is our greenhouse; here we start to grow the people we want—voters who will want us and thus vote for us. Moreover, inasmuch as everyone is for education and what rewards it brings to the individual and society, we never want to present any appearance of not giving the education establishment what they want, and, I might add, this establishment always produces for us. One good turn deserves another.

As you have undoubtedly heard, we are in an envied position when it comes to education, for we are the voice of the poor and the victimized, the disenfranchised, and so on. That is, and in line with everything I have said to you, we never address a potential voter about his own failure as if he or she is the cause. In education it is no different; if our schools are a mess the cause that contributes to the failure never comes close to the individual. Blame must be laid at the point that is most advantageous to us, and furthermore, we never speak of an individual as anything more than a piece of the society in which he lives. By this route, you see, if he fails, it is because society has failed him. If society fails, he fails. We therefore present the obstacles to his success as so mammoth, as so beyond the ken of a single individual to overcome, that we present both success and failure as due to the same thing—society.

One need not worry about the failure thing, however, for it is no ultimate indictment of our effort or lack thereof when it shows up on our watch. We can simply feign ourselves as the failed and now justifiably rebuked steward of our nation's greatest resources—our children. After a suitable period of appropriate and noticeably loud lament for such an atrocity, we start to rattle the coffers and ask for more, that is, more money for education. At this point an opponent is apt to challenge any such financial need for the situation, and this is what you hope he does. In fact, you wait for him. When he has thus laid his neck out for you, you present him to your listeners as a man more concerned with parting with his own money than our children. Ask him how much of his undoubtedly ill-gotten gain is an innocent child worth?

Dear Purefoy,

Yes, you have it, I think. We are social thinkers; even the thought processes of the "individual" are grounded and enclosed in his social milieu and while that thought is too much for the understanding of the ignorant voter, by it we convey to him that an individual at odds with society is at odds with us, and therefore ultimately himself, since "community" makes us all one. By this tact, we are able to silence any troublemaker who goes against us. That is, his thoughts and his criticism show that his lack of sympathies for our causes is due to his own selfishness. He has made himself larger than the society that has produced him; we shall not run out on him, however, as he inevitably would on us; public scorn can work quiet well for us to bring him back into line, or into oblivion.

You might think that a society such as ours would never produce such an individual, that is, one who dares rear his head above others. This is a grave misconception, and one that must be carefully understood and thereafter monitored. To the degree that our tactics work there will be less of such people, because people will wear down from the obstacles of our bureaucratic state and our attempt to enforce equality will meet with fewer and fewer resistors. At the same time, the individual is by nature different in significant degrees from his fellows, and the attempt to ensure and enforce equality will require something of a command structure to guarantee it.

The way we will accomplish our goal in public, therefore, will be to treat people differently based on their differences, but claiming that this must be done so as to achieve equality. Equality will show itself as the ultimate goal because you can justify well nigh everything with a respected goal at your helm and few will see just how radical it is, carried to our goal of a total reconstruction of society. One need not bother with the detractors, however, for equality—and its shoulder word, justice— are very much in vogue these days. We can make just about any opponent run like a scared rabbit by charging him with either of the opposites.

Dear Purefoy,

Yes, we are utopians. The voting public need never hear the word; they only need to know that we can right well nigh every wrong done to them. You see, this is our proof to them that we are for them, by the fact that we can do most anything they have need of. Yes, we are preaching a possible heaven, but remember where it will be—here, and it is we who can give and we who can take it away.

The savvy opponent must be carefully dealt with here, for he may charge your utopian dream with elements of fantasy, but this charge is not as formidable as it might seem. You can simply ask him what reality he wishes for us to accept: starving children, soldiers shoveled off to war, conniving landlords, injustice, inequality—you get the idea. You see by this tact you can push him into being seen as an old establishment curmudgeon who will let problems continue to be problems. Further, and as I said before, you can make him look like a cruel barbarian to your voters. Don't miss this opportunity, and it will come along for you many times. Don't waste any chances, and where such opportunities are lacking, create them.

Dreams and visions are your token words, and they will catch the voters, especially after your voters see that your talk of dreams and visions is for them and that you deliver. Of course we cannot do everything, but you never tell the voter what you cannot do, but what you can. To effect this you make our voter look at you as more than simply his employee—indeed, as his god. He pays you with his vote, which costs him nothing; you repay him by providing goods and services. Lest the equation sound too economic, you can simply explain that you are his public servant. Your role toward meeting his private needs will be to turn them all into public needs, which will be met by government, and thus will guarantee his vote for you and no one else.

Our opponents, on the other hand, must be portrayed as playground bullies standing between the playground and the people. One of our major functions is therefore to protect and defend our citizens against these bullies. With all the zeal with which our opponents are prepared to fight "enemies" abroad, we will pick and fight our enemies here at home. This is to our great advantage; the voter is always more cognizant of his own condition and household than he is of anything in a country separated from him by an ocean or two.

Of late we have seen a version of these same postures played out in the case of the so-called "illegals." In this case, a portion of the population of a neighboring country is in our country and our opponent wants to push and shove them all back to the poverty from which they came, and from which they had hoped to escape. This creates another mammoth opportunity for us to show our infinite generosity and our humanity. Remember, the playground bullies must be depicted as manifesting none of either of our qualities. We therefore welcome the "illegals," asserting, as some of our sloganeering has it, "no human is an 'illegal.'" You see this makes our opponent appear to regard our neighbor to the south as having more significance in his status as an "illegal," than in his status as a human being. Furthermore, our opponent places the law above humans; we will have none of that natural law stuff, and will quote the words of one of their own, that the law was made for man, not man for the law. You see, religion is once again not the enemy you first imagine, but another resource for the humiliating rebuke of our opponents.

So you see we now are the able defender of the downtrodden who previously followed protocol and sailed into Ellis Island and did paperwork, but now must swim a river or climb a wall we have erected to keep them out. Tell—I mean shout—at your opponent, that it is time for a nation to do some serious soul-searching when it can throw back people who have exerted that kind of effort to come to our land. If the guilty one is religious tell him to repent, and that we will do the work of welcoming our guests while he apologizes and begs forgiveness for not wanting them in the first place.

We must give every indication that we are prepared to put a new leaf in the kitchen table to make it bigger for our guests, who are ultimately to be made citizens like ourselves, but at diminished costs thanks to our generosity. This exuded generosity will stymie our cantankerous opponent, and if he has anything left in his quiver it will be the arrow he always brings out in every debate like this. You know what that is already, because I have told you often. He will lament the costs. I have also told you how to respond to a quibble over money when humans are involved. If you do that correctly, the crowd will finish him off because you will have delivered your opponent into arms as unwelcoming as his folded and unextended arms were toward our neighbors to the south.

Dear Purefoy,

It is not just a border wall we deplore; we refrain from issuing labels for any humans except our political opponents. For example, like the institution headquartered in New York City, which, by the way, we should be taking orders from instead of our own provincial government, we will not define "evil." Meanwhile our opponent splashes the word around the world describing various other countries of the world—forgetting his own for once—and incurs their justified wrath. We have many willing accomplices in the press and various organizations scattered about sharing our reluctance to not judge that we be not judged, so we are not alone, and remember, we hate the alone thing. This kind of posturing can swoon the hesitating voter into voting in your favor because you give him an exhibition of pious humility.

Doing it is not all that difficult. Refuse to look upon any adversary—except your political opponent of course—as not convertible to your way of thinking. To do this, we must exhibit no fear of frankly human monsters, and the voting audience that witnesses this pious undertaking will see that you have something that few in the world—maybe next to none—can claim. So whereas our opponent will call out his soldiers to wreck havoc on belligerents, we treat them as if they have no history of misbehaving. We treat them as the gentleman they are not, to cause them to become the gentleman they are. You see, to our opponent we look duped, but to our belligerent we look saintly. Stymied by our consoling rather than condemning the belligerent, the "belligerent" becomes a saint like you, and now you and he can both work together against your political opponent. Meanwhile, your opponent who would identify evil, and have the temerity to call it by name, finds himself with a new dilemma—your new friend. If you play this hand skillfully, you may even get your new friend—though he be separated by an ocean or more from you and may in fact be putting out his own soldiers against those of your allies elsewhere—to endorse you as the preferred candidate in your bid for election. So now the enemy of your true enemy, your political opponent, has become your friend.

Meanwhile, do not worry if this creates too much mess; we cannot win every election, and we need our opponent to clean up the messes sometimes. Thus, the fact that he wins an election every so often is needful for us. In effect, we cannot lose, even when we lose. Only we are not going to lose the upcoming election.

Dear Purefoy,

Our opponent must have an opponent, and this desire for hostility is fed by his foreign policy, by which he habitually looks for reasons to go to war. In addition, it enables him to swagger about, as he talks about the need to go into all parts of the world to bring his gun against "evil." We, who recognize no evil in the world sufficient to raise up any army, appear always ready for reconciliation rather than mobilization for war. We therefore come across to the voter as likeable and friendly and able to resolve various crises in the world without so much as raising our voice. Instead of killing, we befriend our enemy and his whole nation, by persuading him to lay down his arms because we never took ours up.

Another advantage to us in this matter is that our opponent's foreign opponent is for the most part never seen up close by the voter; he is not, for example, stalking and peeking in homes around the city. He remains therefore an abstraction to the voter who is warned about him by your opponent. The belligerent might as well be in another world—which he is. There is therefore no need to confront such an enemy, except in the most extraordinary circumstances.

Yes, that time may come, but when it does, we can still work the situation to our advantage. Like one of our own did only a few years ago—employing the tactics of delay through dialogue—he bought off evil long enough to keep the peace on his watch, which erupted quite otherwise very soon into our opponent's watch. Therefore our opponent inherited the problem, which is as we would have it, if a conflict is inevitable.

Yes, these matters can become delicate at times, but do not fret. There is always a maneuver possible in order to shift your burdens onto your opponent and for him to have to deal with it—to the point that the voter will yearn to go back to the peaceable years—and thus we can be reelected when the messiness is over and the problem resolved.

Thus we have an enemy, though he is not some foreign despot, but rather our political opponent. Combat with him requires no weapons but a few pithy phrases and jokes and lifted eyebrows and the skewered tone of voice. Make him look the fool that he is, or better, make him agonize in the knowledge of how easily you are defeating a man defeated by his own incomprehension of your tactics. As I said some time before, save for losing elections more than we actually do, one would wish for a political race in which one's opponent presented more of a challenge. At times the sliding board is just too easy. Oh well, tomorrow is another day.

Dear Purefoy,

Yes, the riches of religion are not less rich for irreligious folk such as us. You see this is where the unknowing among our ranks miss an opportunity. They perceive that because we are striving for a state that is secular in terms of law or forms, the religious amongst potential voters cannot be courted. Indeed, they must be courted and not given to the wiles of the opposition.

Religion is our enemy, but the religious voter can be converted to our thinking with a bit of ingenuity on our part. First, and above all, and never forget it, we must present ourselves as the fulfillment of the Christian religion. This may sound odd to you, but in fact it presents us with extraordinary opportunity, nearly as good as that accomplished by miracles of the religion of old. Because of our deeds we can bring a recalcitrant religious population to us. We do this by bringing them around to the view that our good deeds express their own religion in action.

Initially, it may be hard going—but, be advised, it can be done. In the beginning, moreover, one must find one's way into their pulpits, because this is where these people are—they are not out on the pavement, as we and ours are, tending to the powerless, from which we ultimately derive and maintain our power.

You see, these people live under the tutelage of their pulpiteers, so you must find some way to get yourself to that bully pulpit. This may be the hardest thing to do, and in many cases it requires an inside connection. That being said, get yourself to that pulpit by hook or slither, but in your sermon take the pew-sitters away from where they are, to where you are. That is, speak of the dispossessed, the oppressed, the downtrodden, the have-nots, the disenfranchised. You see, these unfortunates are talked about in their revered book; quote some of the holy snippets to make your point, and then forget their book and instead move on and go for their votes. Tell them one cannot simply talk the talk, but one must walk the talk and without harm to our dear Mother Earth. And then ever so carefully coax them into seeing that their Bread of Life is bread itself. You see, their God is Spirit; our god is Matter. Thus, we must convince them that bread matters because life matters, and since life matters we have opportunity to go about providing bread. Tell them that the communion table still matters, but the kitchen table matters most. Exercise extreme care here. Nevertheless, phrase your words ever so boldly and with the fire of the prophetic utterance.

Undoubtedly, some of your listeners may be thinking of a roast they have in their oven at that very moment and the feast that is theirs after you quit talking. Then they anticipate going home to eat what is theirs. But because you have talked about empty tables, they know with pangs of guilt how full their own table is, and because your speech is working, their guilt escalates and will draw them to you and what you are saying about the way they live, which is ultimately about the way they vote.

Now you are poised to change them. Tell them they are thinking about their full tables, but you have simply reminded them of the empty ones.

Dear Purefoy,

Yes, different tactics are necessary among different voters who are religious. Amongst the one group, but one certainly expanding in this country in the past half century, your message of materialism will further advance them toward secularism. This is because "deacons" in such churches are more used to waiting on tables than they are wailing beneath their crosses. Nevertheless, to strengthen your grip on the voter in this group, one must persuade him to spend even less time on bent knees and encourage him to stand upright and solidly on his secular feet. To do this his thought about his "sin," probably already nearly vanquished, must nevertheless be brought to a juggernaut, a table of judgment: the kitchen table. Convince him that no gatekeepers of the church should accept the penitent until the poor have their plenty.

The other religious group may be harder going for vote getting, but they are slipping and sliding in our direction, and better yet, have hardly noticed their steady and secular drift. In former decades representatives of this group could pick away and some even challenge our argument for reversing the traditional ordering of preachers and deacons. Part of their ability to challenge us was imparted to them by the training and knowledge of their touted book.

Some time ago, however, when some among them decided their churches resembled more a marketplace than a sacred place, they made it into the former, and prodded it more and more in a secular direction, though of course with little thought of consequences. Even their precious pulpit, previously the fount of endless touting of the afflictions of men estranged from God, has become the font of therapy sessions, with their god made to serve them.

Yes we are the party of the belly: the kitchen table, as I said before. This is an object lesson because it is a place visited three times a day. Every missed meal is an opportunity for your potential voter to think of your assurance that anything missing on that table is our concern.

Dear Purefoy,

Yes, every time our opponents intimate or even suggest going on the military warpath again, bring up the shameful colonialism of the past. Of course, our allies across the water have a more shameful record of that than we, but the brethren across the water have for some time now shown no interest in resurrecting an old vice, whereas our penchant for meddling in the affairs of others shows renewed signs of energy. Of course, the guilty—our political opponents—drape all such ventures in a flag, or worse, that word freedom, but we have chastened them for some time now with their dismal record of war of late. We, for our part, don't mind if our voters burn the flag rather than take it into battle; it shows our respect for the independence of our voters to do what they will, and gives them the impression that we will support and defend anyone who will support us.

In that sense, we are the true Americans of this vast piece of real estate between the Atlantic and Pacific. Americans have always shown their radicalness and their outrage; the sixties was an all-American decade. For our opponents, of course, the sixties were a meltdown. Of course they were, but in the sense of advantage to us who want to turn the country upside down in our favor.

It is turning and is about to turn full circle. Now the warmongering of our despicable past is resisted by our protests in the street and in mass by our voters. By such displays, we can bring whole armies home, shamed of their shameful fight with pretended aggressors. You see, and as the latest cultural critique of warmongering portends, it is just a matter of time before war becomes a thing of the past and that piece of the latest cultural property and achievement will belong to us. No mother wants her sons traipsing off to killing-fields. What her grandmother, indeed her mother, had to witness, in giving up sons to the spilling of blood, will never be seen again, and the reward of that blessing will be our political philosophy in permanent power.

Dear Purefoy,

We detest war and will not have recourse to one. We may have to delay an inevitable conflict so that it is our opponents who must dirty their hands with a problem we divert to them. This can be effected quite easily as the voter believes in our image as one who resolves conflicts with words, not with weapons of violence. Of course, with any external enemy for which our words constitute no protection from his bullets, we simply delay meeting the bullets until our political opponents are in office, and they can do the messy work of war in our absence.

That difficulty, of course, means that we simply cannot be in office all the time. This fact is a bit of realism we have to face, but even if it sends us out of office occasionally, as soon as we return we can return to our old message, and tell the voters that if we had been in power, we could have negotiated an understanding that would have made the war unnecessary. This maneuver is not as irresponsible as it may appear because the truth of the matter is that there is less and less need for war in our increasingly civilized world, and thus the need we have for our political opponents will disappear when the wars disappear.

Yes, the wars will dissipate, as we have begun to see for some years now, and then, however slowly, go away. So the need for our political opponent to clamor and thrash about in need of an enemy to go to war with—all the time showing his resolve to "defend" the country—will simply be eventually unnecessary and finally anachronistic. He will be seen as a cave man, with his club and all, and we will be seen for the truly enlightened people that we are. Remember we are the politicians of the dinner table, and people will always have to eat. They need not ever go to war with us in office. Our opponent who exists to meddle in the affairs of houses not his own, and across vast oceans, will in time have no reason to "bring the peace," because it will come without him. Then, unlike us, he will have no reason to be.

Neither do we have to do all the work to expedite this coming warless world. The people, as indicated by the mounting protests over our recent warmongering, are decreasingly ready to fight in any war, and when we affirm their point of view with a few more adjectives than they, they line up behind us to vote for us. Remember, you do not want to disrupt the dinner table. In fact, you can use that table to make your point about no time or need for war. That is, instead of meeting our foreign "opponent" with a weapon, extend to him an invitation to dinner. Even some of your sympathetic listeners will not have taken their own protest over war and compliments to the "enemy" that far, and when they hear you utter such an invitation, they will be convinced that anybody who could make such a gesture to a scoundrel must be a saint. Once again, you exhibit your deep religiosity to the religious among our voters.

Indeed, to further solidify the point, quote a little of their religious text to the doubters—about heaping coals of fire on an opponent—and, I dare say, any listener who suspects you as the party of the irreligious will never again entertain that thought and will being ashamed for ever having had the idea about you. That day he will have found a new shepherd, one that he has grossly misread for a long time, and thus he will give up his old shepherd in the process. Even that switch, however, is not the end of the heights to which your new voter can help you. Having sufficiently swooned him in the direction of your moral compass, remind him of the confusion from which he came. Remind him how our opponent proposes to save babies from the abortionist's tools, only to confirm the lethal injection to the inmates. This will let your voter know that our opponent makes an incorrect distinction, such that he can save the "innocent" and kill the "guilty" and call himself moral for both.

A contentious opponent, of course, will challenge you, but you have nothing to fear from an opponent who treats his enemies like unreformable criminals. You remember all the hype they got from their "three strikes you're out" campaign some time ago. Once again, quote their own text to them; tell them three times is not enough, that it will have to be seven times nine hundred. Your opponent will scarcely be able to speak, and not because he cannot calculate the product of that multiplier. Indeed, if the audience is disposed in your favor, tell him that forgiveness will only stop with an infinite number, and they may admonish him for you. Nevertheless, so as to never waste a single opportunity, save him from the stoners in your audience, and for this rescue from an early death he may stay at your side permanently.

Dear Purefoy,

Yes, you will invariably hear the opponent clamoring endlessly about the "rule of law." Here again you can quote one of their heroes about law made for men, not men made for law, but sooner or later, you will hear talk about our nation being a nation of laws and not of men. Indeed we are; but we are the men who made the laws. It is therefore we who are in charge of laws, and not the reverse. We are running and promulgating laws; laws are not making us. I must insist upon obedience to this dictum, for our opponents sound as if their notion of law is derivative from that of Zeus or Thor. This is a scary, indeed, a terrifying notion, for by it our opponents would bring heaven to earth; I mean, oh yes, a theocracy. Except, of course, their absentee god would rule by abstention, placing his most obedient flesh and blood in charge so that we could be obedient to the terrestrial tyrant, who, in turn, will be obedient to the celestial tyrant. It is a fairy tale without a happy ending; our job is to make sure it never comes to fruition.

Our notion of law—which must be worded carefully so as not to provoke the mob to turn vigilante on us—is that we make it up as we go along. There is no heavenly tablet from which our law on the ground is to derive. Our laws are of the ooze from which we came and to which we shall return. Gravity is with us now and will be then. We aren't going up because we came from below, and to below we shall return. You take us upwards far enough, and we either freeze or suffocate; we never lived there nor were we meant to and our laws do not come from there anymore than we did. Laws came and will come from us; there will be no law after us, for there was no law before us.

That is our position, and mark it well; teach it to your sons and daughters, and teach them to teach it to their children.

You see law is not made in front of us, but after us. We are the measure of all things and this is the safe and humane position. We oversee ourselves without oversight, and this is why, with justification, we rise above our fellows: in their interests of course.

Our laws come from below and behind, and in time, with sufficient care, can be brought to the front to govern with. The heavenly law, the law from on high as the pious speak of, is murderous. Our law has no such intention; it brings peace, not war, not violence. It keeps us alive as best it can, and keeps us away from smoke, both manmade and natural, so that we can live upon this planet as long as the air is clear and clean. Our causes do not rise much above that and clean water, but that is sufficient for now, though of course we do not live lives with even a pinch of the excitement of yesteryear.

Were it not for the opponents we have, which give us reason to be, we would have no excitement, for we are fear mongers, and yes, we are risk averse. And it has taken a toll on us, but the masses need not be told, nor I dare say have many even noticed. A kitchen table outfitted with what sits on a table will keep most contented for quite some time. No mountains to climb—only tables to furnish. We are only too happy to accommodate, but there was a time when we lived for greater challenges and obstacles. We of course did not gleefully scamper about to find them, but when they came within our vision our cultural adrenaline rose. With that escalation, the obstacle scarcely looked so formidable as to cause us to shudder and hide with paralyzing fear.

Now we encourage fear, and we have so eliminated the discomforts of life that we are constantly inventing new ones, claiming ones that are not, and all so that we have something coming at us, so that we have reason to arise the next morning.

Dear Purefoy,

Perverting justice should be apparent. A word like justice already gets a safe pass whenever we use it; to even suggest a challenge to our meaning for the word today is to create an appearance of desiring injustice. You should therefore use such words often, for they provide a shield for you.

When you find your opponent starting to mimic you, then you know that he knows that he is losing. He cannot, as I have told you before, beat us at our own game. You know that he knows you own the ideas and the strategies to win, when he by theft attempts to steal them. Steal them he may, but he will never be able to keep them because he can never deliver more of them than we. Remember, we will open the spigots of government as wide as the revolutions required to never say no to our captive voters who in time will be permanently ours. When your opponent is simply copying you, you can feel confident that he cannot catch or overtake you. It is impossible. Should he by some fluke happen to do that, don't take him as your fool anymore, simply take him under your wing. You must be very selective, however; we cannot extend the hand of welcome to everyone.

The disenfranchised are valuable capital for us for this reason, and so we never want to be rid of them, for with them we can wag our finger every time at our opponent, as being responsible for those neglected members of our society. These neglected citizens must not, however, be merely presented as forgotten, but as the shoved out and oppressed members of society. However, some new tactics are needed, for some of the concoctions I heard from recent campaigns sounded like stories from a century ago, when whole streets of voters on their way to the polls were blocked by highjackers standing in the street to physically impede voters. Much more conceivable in terms of our enemies is some technical sabotage that blocks vote counts in districts likely to vote for us. The sky is the limit on imagining the unimaginable lengths to which our political opponent would scheme to deny the right to vote to voters not voting for him. We, by contrast, enable those who would not and could not vote, to vote.

Dear Purefoy,

By no means do we have to abandon the charge of colonialism against our opponents just because most of it is gone and largely belongs to bygone eras. Since we missed out on virtually all of what our European brothers enjoyed for quite some time, we have lacked as much opportunity to grovel because of such—until now. Thus, you can now charge your opponent with envying the idea, indeed having resented an opportunity he scarcely ever had until now; he only gives it up when the clamor against it becomes too great. Now you see we have already started that charge about empire again, and in doing so, we make our opponent look like a Neanderthal clubbing his way throughout the world.

You understand that we want to portray our opponent in terms of a gun-toting, swashbuckling and kooky cowboy, ready to shoot first and interrogate and torture later. And, as you have surely seen, we have had not a few opponents, who in their style and their actions, fit our caricature to a tee. The more swagger they have, the less intelligence we surmise. The public is a sucker for such portraits of our opponents, and soon you will hear the ignorant masses picking up our ideas about those people unfortunate enough to be our opponents.

Because the thirst for colonialism is now exercising itself with our opponents, we want to portray our allies across the ocean as light years ahead of us; thus, while we are returning to the slime from which we have come, they have moved beyond their past mistakes to a warless world, having little need to colonize anyone anymore, excepting their socialist experiments with their own people. Our opponent, meanwhile, takes his beloved "democracy" to the ends of the earth.

Yes, you will hear our opponents clamor about democracy while toting guns and firing at anything that does not suit them, while also intruding upon other countries and their right to kill their own people. You can begin by telling such an opponent to get off his high horse of platitudes about democracy and then charge him with toting and using his weapons against peoples who want nothing to do with us or our style of government. Of course what we mean by that latter phrase (though of course we refrain from it in most public situations) is that democracy is not for everyone. We never want to appear parochial.

Dear Purefoy,

You undoubtedly witnessed the embarrassment of our opponents this week when they had to fire one of their own, because the man complained about the mass of citizens being complainers. Truth of the matter is that we benefit every way when this happens, because we have made citizens perpetual complainers while presenting ourselves as the only remedy for resolving their complaints. So we need the complainers that our opponent complains about, because we solve the problems precipitating the complaints, while our opponent thrashes about by identifying the problem as the complainer. So you see he serves as a martyr for our cause as he destroys his own. This is because he ignorantly infers that citizens should be ready to scrutinize themselves for their own faults. Our opponent dooms himself by an analysis which makes us rich and him poor at the polls. Remember, we don't tell the people the truth; this was the mistake of the ignorant underling our opposition fired. We tell voters how they can blame someone or something else for their problems. And if they claim they have none or too few problems, which is rarely the case in the culture we have fashioned upon unsuspecting voters, we simply supply them with a list. The list will never end because remember we are utopians; nothing less than imagined heaven on real earth would prompt the endless list of wrongs to be righted to shrivel up.

Of course, no one runs his household effectively by complaining all the time, but we are not running a house, but rather a whole nation that we have taught to complain about everything but their complaining. And we are living off cultural capital built up by prior generations in gargantuan amounts that allow us to pulverize and pillage with no appreciable loss to our immediate selves or the current generation. This tactic presents no loss for us, because future voters don't elect us before they are born, but the living and breathing ones do. Do not forget who the voter is, but at the same time, present various futuristic portends that you use to warn your voter about. Indeed, we can charge our opponent with ruining the current and future world, and here we bring up the future world of the darling grandchildren, and by so doing add to the perception of ourselves as selfless and thinking about others, again. "Future generations," we call it.

The fact of the matter is that we are thieves, plain and simple. We steal in the light of day what someone else worked for for a whole lifetime, day and sometimes night, and in the case of our country, many lifetimes. In other words, the prosperity of the country was built up by the very values that we now denigrate, but the pile of prosperity and cultural capital is so high that we can scoop from the top for a long time before anyone significant notices the pile is dwindling and in time may disappear. We see we are not as selfless as the adoring public thinks.

Examples are not hard to come by. Take the hallowed "freedom" word of our opponents. We care not a bit for it, but the ignorant think we do, because we make civil and legal protests when the opposition starts to talk about surveillance, for example. In fact, we claim our opponent is squeezing and will eventually extinguish the freedom they claim to protect by undermining it with surveillance. The fact of the matter is that freedom must be guarded, and while we clamor that our freedom is being impinged, our opponent guards it for us, while we clamor against him and for freedom. Don't forget the sliding board I have reminded you about. We can have our freedom and destroy it too.

Oh yes, energy costs are escalating, but you need not worry if you notice how much the citizens are complaining over the cost of energy resources. This is our resource, the complaining I mean, and it is infinitely larger than any puddles of lubricant lying under our feet that we prohibit from being brought to the surface. Remember that from this complaining comes our opportunity. So of course we blame the source, which are the producers of energy, particularly if they are profiteers. In the past, and in the present, we haul them into our hallowed congressional halls demanding to see their malicious profit books exposed. You see, we wish all the citizens, I mean voters, to think that businesses should operate as charities, though of course we do not often say so, because some of the voters are business owners. Remember numbers here, however; the owners of business are much fewer than those working for the owners. Remember what I said some time ago: we are not for the little guy, but the more guys.

We can suggest also to the voters that we, the government, take over the resource industry in *toto*. Of course we make them think that in this way they will have better care, because the plundering, gouging profit motive will be abolished. Energy is only the latest opportunity we have for ourselves to extend our base of power, with complaints at near record levels over that stuff that people use as fuel in their cars, but there are others, of course. Health care is another. You see the way it works; keep the complaints coming, by giving the people something to complain about. We then announce ourselves as problem solvers by taking over the problem, when in fact it is we who have significantly provoked the problem, by keeping the profiteers out. By this move we take more and more responsibility away from the people, who are only too glad to give it to us, with little realization what they are giving away. We get what we want, their vote, and they get what we want them to have, and which they do want, for a while anyway—but that is another matter.

So for us bad news is always good news. When there is no bad news, we must create it, though we do not want to come off as pessimists, but the opposite. The way we handle the balancing act is to announce the depression or quagmire we are in, and then to announce the way out, which is to flee to our waiting arms. Those arms are always in the form of a life jacket without which the one in peril will drown. So we announce a bail-out—you get the idea. After a while the people will come to see that when they go it alone, they always end up with problems. We are only too ready to assume responsibility for them if they will only favor us in November.

Dear Purefoy,

Yes, there is much to learn from any of your fellow aspirants to office, both do's and do not's. The trip to see the family in Europe was a big gamble, but a necessary one. Because the stakes were so high for a risk like this, I count the trip a success if no appreciable costs are paid, that is, votes lost for this venture. So far nothing seems to have fallen off the tight rope, though I witnessed some dangerous tilts. We lost no previously committed votes in going across the Atlantic and indeed gained a few from the undecided, while provoking the demented hatred of our domestic enemies into a rant that our politics belong to Europe and not to America.

Of course, no European can cast a vote for us: that was not the reason for this trip. The trip over was for almost persuaded voters back home who needed to hear things that could only be said there, but not here. There we talk openly about wealth redistribution, boiling down all picks for welfare check openers, four weeks mandatory vacation, disarmament, frisking the rich and so on. Our almost persuaded voter back home then knows that we truly want to remake the country in the image of our socialist brethren, but this rankles those patriot types who insist that we left them ages ago and should not seek their backing.

These sniffing people, like the dogs you see in the airports, are menacing to our cause, but they are relatively few in number, and remember we are after the most voters, not the fewer voters. That being said, these fewer are on the hunt for our candidates and hence must be thrown off our trail. This was one reason we went to Europe and said what was said there and not here. At the same time we had to provide enough smoke to make our words seem at least patriotic in miniature toward our own nation—for those majority voters back home—but all the while we rhapsodize about the heavenly state of Europe and then whisper that it is a union where none fare as badly as the bottom forty million Americans.

So as not to offend our hosts we make no mention of the embarrassing wealth of our country. When we encounter a frown over our wealth from the brethren, we respond by intimating that it must be dispensed with by government as it was greedily made in the private sector. For our future administration only the noblest motives will chart a course for a country we will make anew, in which the private sector will have less and less to say about everything, and government will take the place of greed. With this look to the future of America, the brethren of course looked favorably upon us, and thus the American voter who wants his country remade in the socialist image also saw everything needful to now trip the trigger for us in November, and it is only August. Thus, this was the reason for our little trip over; that was a success.

There are those who are now more adamant to not vote for us and will now try to persuade others to do the same. They are not the almost persuaded voter I mentioned before, but the voter of which I now speak recognizes that our politics are not theirs and never will be. In other words, they see us leaning hard, though not backwards but forward. Our savviest opponents saw that they now have their work cut out for them: convincing their own to not cross over and vote for us.

The rest of the voters are too ignorant and simply think we went over there for some good-will gesture or to sightsee. More about them later.

One might say here, then, that the added votes and the lost votes cancel each other, thus making the trip of no net gain, but this is a mistake. The hard to sway and smart voters have been satisfied and decided their vote three months early—we can reasonably forget about them now, because our attention is needed elsewhere. The masses beckon for our gifts, as we beckon for their votes, and silver tongues assure them of timely distribution as soon as they pull the voting lever for us.

Of the large and ignorant masses, our standard procedure will insure their votes without question. Nevertheless, we must repeat and repeat and repeat our promises. These masses understand little but their kitchen table, as I told you before. Therefore, you, as well as all of our candidates, should cry that a wolf is at the door, and that you are the only possible protector and that that task will be accomplished without a single shot, for you will outlaw all weapons. In presenting this picture of yourself and our platform it helps that the opposition has been in power for some years, because you can paint a picture of the country as dour as you dare. Portray the world as about to collapse and that you and we will act as the rescue party. Meals, mortgagers, and everything else will be taken care of.

You see how we ever so discretely, at least most of the time, intimate that our own country is about to collapse, should we not be elected. Our trip to Europe presented us as already in office; such a move deflects any doubt about our confidence. You know hope is one of our words, and we are skillful at the heavenly associations of that daring word. However, few of our European brethren, or we for that matter, believe in that religious stuff. We are nevertheless happy to be secular saviors coming off the street rather than down from the skies. People don't care where their food comes from, up or down, just as long as it comes. Nor do they care from whence their leader came. Devil or deity makes no matter to them as long as they get what they desire.

Your own campaign can take a few lessons from what you witnessed. There will, of course, be need for a few tweaks because of the distance we unfortunately have from them, being in the social backwater of the west compared to the Europeans. Here in America, touted as the land of the free, fewer and fewer are enjoying any wine or palatable food as prices force them to eat the simpler meals, but even these are growing out of reach of many who see their food going for fuel, while both skyrocket in price. You tell them that famine is around the corner if our opposition wins the election.

All this our brethren in Europe provide for from cradle to casket. Enough said.

Our ignorant masses are strangers to big words, so don't use them when you are among them, not even medium words, like "income-redistribution"—but food and gasoline and cable television and the like they understand perfectly well. Frankly, if you talk about these "issues" to your voters, and talk about them well, which means promising more of these things for them, they will give you the votes you need to get these goods to them. Enough said again. Now start practicing what I have been preaching. If your polling numbers do not rise I will know you have not been reading these letters sufficiently.

Dear Purefoy,

You are making this campaign too difficult by listening to your "conscience" when you should be listening to your voters and their wants; remember, the voters elect us to office, so do not debate the dubiousness of your promises to the voters, nor the prompts from them that evoke your promises. Instead think of your future office as dependent upon voters and you getting them by making the voter dependent on you. Remember above all that you will get the office because of your skill of grandiose visions, posturing, feigning, and anything else required. Make the expectations of the voter seem realized in you. So come off your high horse to a little political reality. That reality is that the shortest way to the office you aspire to is through the voter who will put you there. Present him with a list of what you will do for him, everything from taking care of the maternity bill to the mortgage payment to lawn seed and mortuary matters. Then he will flock to you, possibly with all his neighbors in tow. If you do a superb job, your exuberant voter-follower may put a sign up in his neighborhood that no citizens of the opponent's persuasion are welcome in his neighborhood. We already have yard signs telling trains to reroute themselves if they are carrying that planet-destroying coal through our towns; to contemplate the former is not therefore unthinkable. Remember, all things are political—even our front yards.

Of course, the poorer among your voters we can always count on, because they always count on us, but remembering that, you must go out and create more of them because of it. Second, you must impugn the pinnacled citizens above them as responsible for the poverty below them. You contribute to the guilt of the guilty for their gargantuan gain by a constant harangue of charges that this tiny group is composed of gorged parasites feeding off the multitudinous members of society beneath them. You can use some of our old stock phrases. For example, that wealth is built on the backs of our lower classes, our seniors, and our youth and everyone in between. And you have double advantage in the fact that the wealthy have so much wealth and at the same time constitute such a small group of people. Thus, you can impugn their exorbitant wealth for all others to envy with everybody except the rich coming to hate the rich. Here we are sometimes so convincing, that even a handful of the dastardly rich will come out for us because we have been so convincing with our message of wealth and success as evil. You need not worry over the votes of the other rich lost because you portray them as villainous, for they are a miniscule group. You lose one or two votes of the guilty for every hundred or so of those gained from everybody else.

Of course, an even better bit of news is that the conditions are improving for a socialist revolution in our country. Our candidates do not drop that word—we still have a few years before we can use it in public places—though detractors are using it about some of our candidates. They, of course, cannot make it stick because we have so much camouflage around us. We therefore use code language, such as our most current and laudatory phrase, "social justice." We, in other words, are levelers with contempt for social ladders and wealth.

You need not worry yourself with anything beyond what I have mentioned in these letters to get elected; this is substance enough. The substance is that the voter puts you in office. What the voter wants is therefore what you promise him for his vote. If he doesn't know, tell him, and assume the perspective of a child who believes in the tooth fairy and Santa. Your lists of his wants can create more poor—the so-called poor who don't know they are poor—but more importantly new converts who start to think about you as the giver from government. Indeed, they need to come away with the impression that you can give so much that charity will no longer be needed, or, as amongst some of our European brethren, outlawed as a wrongful private competitor against government giving. The real poor need the necessities. Guarantee them. The not-so-poor need more beyond the necessities. Inform them of what they can be and guarantee them. The middle class needs even more. Guarantee it. The wealthy do not need anymore. Take what they have to give to the rest. So, talk about equality as if you favored it, and do with it as you want.

Everything else is style. Getting elected is as simple as the way you package yourself. I mean look at your models; they project themselves now as what they will be in the future. Of course our detractors marshal the charge of arrogance, but we are simply preparing the voters to vote for us. Our opposition has little notion of the voters. If our candidates act a bit pretentious, as the Hollywoods do, just remember that your voters are apt to know Hollywood better than Washington. Therefore the tilt toward glamour for the eyes it attracts is to our gain. Thus, our opponent who thought the ad linking our candidates with the brainless Hollywoods detrimental to us will find in time that the presumed damaging ad will rebound to the popularity of our candidates. Thus, our candidates show their savvy with voters by positioning themselves with the people types they know best and admire most. If we act otherwise, I mean typical, average, bland, yes and no, good and bad, black and white, they would have no liking for us and would have every reason to doubt us. If we portray ourselves with grandiose confidence, as in a sense not one of them, perhaps even as a winged figure of sorts, but prepared to work for earthlings, then they have the candidates they want, indeed, can worship. You have seen the godless media fawning over our number; imagine the treatment the godly voter will bestow upon our gods—needed votes to the office our candidates aspire!!

Remember, again, getting elected is about giving the people what they want, but more pointedly stated, what they have been denied. This presents them not as humble beggars, but as demanding citizens. You simply steer their wants in the direction of wanting more. And then, as they start to do this, you step in front of them and fill out the utopian vision in ways they have not dreamed of—yet. You denounce your opponent as you dream for your voters. Then you let voters know that their lack of such a dream was not for lack of their imagination. Rather, the lack was because of political opponents who loved money more than people and therefore never allowed the people to dream our dream of everything for everybody.

Dear Purefoy,

Our opponents have plundered the earth since the rise of the middle class and the Scientific and Industrial Revolutions that came in their wake. Today, however, is a new day, our day, and it is one in which we can catalog the ills that have afflicted us and our planet because of our opponent's shameful history of lust for money and power. Our opponents stole political power from our predecessors at court through alliance with legislatures and parliaments during this lengthy drought within our history. The usurpers made themselves richer at the expense of the rest of us and the pain of the planet, but now is our time, as our candidates have put it. The time is nearly ripe for our aspiring bureaucracy, patterned after that of our European brethren. We shall need a powerful leader, a man of the world, so to speak, to put the authority in place to have a new country. Our candidates, of course, claim to want to return the country to yesteryear, but there is no yesteryear of our country corresponding to the direction in which our politics will move our country. However much your own campaign has faltered, perhaps you shall be so lucky as to ride into office on the robes of the rest of us.

You should see by now that we care little for freedom, except our own, but the ignorant have no clue about our subversive ploys, especially while we are telling them that we are the advocates for participatory democracy, as we call it. Our ignorant masses we manipulate well when we tell them government is meant to serve the people, because of course we have no belief in the fitness of the people to rule anything, not even their own household, much less their own money. On the other hand, tax rebates and the like are affronts to those who are prepared to sacrifice some of their plenty so that the poor can climb out of poverty. Meanwhile, as I said in my last letter, make sure you are adding to the numbers of those needing the climb up by every statistical count you can manage. If there are none, invent some new kind of statistics. If you cannot do it yourself, find help in the academy; there are plenty of our own there and in Hollywood too, ready to bring about our new epoch.

Remember that wolf we keep telling the voter about, the one that is hiding in the shrubbery or out in the woods, and only too ready to vandalize cupboards. Tell the voter that the wolf is waiting for them to drop their guard—that is, they may wrongly think that they can manage the wolf by their own devices. Dissuade them of any protection they may think they have, such as anything that we disparage as "private."

Remember too, that the public must think of our opponent as offering them only two choices—sink or swim. We offer one—floating, and we will supply the raft and weapons (but not guns) for the sharks in the waters. Let your voter know that no shark is as savage as your opponent, and force on your opponent the admission that his politics are squeezing every man to fend for himself, for this leaves the impression that many will be left to drown or freeze or starve at the hands of our beneficent Mother Earth, lest we politicians intervene. If you portray his future with this kind of horror, he will come on his knees to you. This will make it easier to check to see if he has money or arms that he must hand over to you. Then you will have him in your pocket after checking his, and then you can provide him with virtually every other essential, and some not-so-essentials, so that he cannot walk away. Set him up on an allowance, like a child, and he will never leave home. His ventures and any adventures he had in the past will stay put. You are now in charge of him.

Remember, by keeping the poor poor, the poor can never leave nor forsake us; they can only return to you and to us—or starve. With you he is safe; without you he is dead. Of course do not present this scenario in such ribald terms, but do convey the catastrophe that awaits a wrong choice. Nine times out of ten he will run to you as a child would under a similar warning, except your child is an adult who can vote! The tenth we do not worry about; one does not need to worry when 10 sheep are lost if 90 are in the corral. Remember, we are not about the few, but the many.

We have therefore been trying to wrestle as much control as we can back from the people who took it from us after the downfall of the court, with their markets and every sort of egoism that produced a world and a country that we detest. We, of course, portray ourselves as minded by the spirit of community, rather than the selfishness of the individual ego.

If the people are not close enough to starvation for the wolf at the door thing to work, try mentioning killing the planet for more pessimism. Here you can drag up centuries of wrongdoing against our opponent who is now willing to continue plundering earth for gain until Mother has nothing left to give, as She dies and ourselves with Her. Our gentle caress of nature, rather than a rabid brutalizing of our sacred Mother, will appeal to those voters who prefer peace to war, and who sense that everything our opponent does occurs with a hand of violence.

Our judges will do it quite well for us too. By the vote of these few individuals the will of the whole country can be subjugated to our agenda. For our part, we have little care whether we rule from the bench or the throne, as long as we rule. One court is as good as another, whether it is that of a king or a judge. This necessitates, however, that our dearest judges be appointed by one of our own, for there is nothing as onerous as watching a dead political opponent live on through his judicial appointees.

We rule from the top down; our opponent will contend that rule should come from the bottom and go up. He therefore has belief in all sorts of movement and mobility that we either shun or prohibit or pronounce impossible or impious. We are fatalists, though not in name. We offer opportunity, but opportunity which provides opportunity for us to be elected. You must convince your voter that he can do next to nothing about his circumstances, and that his circumstances will take political action to move. Meanwhile, and to your advantage, he will lie about and grow obese, and then require some intervention to rescue him from the predicament you have built for him for yourself.

Dear Purefoy,

In debate a few essentials are worth keeping in mind. Because you need voters your appeal will have to be to the majority of them. Therefore, beware of too much clarity that might exclude a voting bloc that you need. Remember too that we are seeking to lead the group to us and not the solitary individual. The individual has one vote, the many have many more. As such, though we tout the lonely prophetic voice crying in the wilderness, and though we pretend to be as if we were him, we in fact are seeking to congregate individuals around other individuals to the point that the single dot cannot be seen for the maze of faceless masses that can put us in office. Thus, we are for the masses. The word has such a sound of work and fatigue and oppression about it, thanks to us. Furthermore, we want dissent and difference silenced, and nothing like the roar of a crowd—our crowd mind you—can better smother the single voice. We haven't been for the individual for a generation now.

Your entire adage about "plain talk" to the voter that you speak of is garbage. No voter wants "plain talk" anymore than he wants to be told a truth that might offend or anger him. This plain talk, if you mean by it exaggeration of the truth so that the point is plain, is permissible as long as you are plain talking about your opponent in ways that make him averse to the voter. But beware of letting your speech be yes and no. With only two alternatives, one is apt to show too much commitment to too little. The voters, remember, are not little—not the ones that elect you—but the most voters. Therefore, in casting your net for the most of them, you must stretch yourself to accommodate as many of them as you can. Sit on the fence until you have enough votes that you need not sit there anymore, because they voted for you and now you can go home—or, I mean, to your newly elected office!!

This is not difficult. The voter is not swooned by "plain talk," as you imagine, but profundity, which is really not that of course, but instead nothing more than potion you work up to feed to him. He will eat it because of you and because your profundity swoons him into ingesting your words, which of course are too deep for him—as the ignorant masses will confess from their knees. Meanwhile, not plain or "straight talk" but nuance is what the voter likes these days.

Nuance is as attractive to the human mind as a woman's cleavage is attractive to the male eye. Both blind the onlooker to the lesser qualities masked by the glamour of the surface. Drawn by the tip of an iceberg, a covered mass that reflects the depths of what little is seen, the audience will linger for more. Not clarity, but clutter of the right kind is what you want. The opponent's clarity will show and reveal his lack of sophistication at this game of getting listeners and with it voters, for he lacks the ability to see the complex in his entire clamor for clarity about the issues, as he is want to say. By the sleight of hand of the nuance, you will have governance in your hand next, for the world is too complicated for simpletons such as your opponent to grasp. Your opponent is truly talking about a world of fairy tales, where there are good and bad guys, but you are between them, dialoguing, to use one of our favorite words, and one loved by our beloved listeners, who are in speechless mystic awe at our ability to maneuver in a sea where we cannot discern the difference between darkness and light.

If pressed by your opponent, of course, you are not cornered, because you have all the slippery character that nuance allows. So, you tell him, much as one of our flourishing candidates intimated in his own debate only days ago, that if darkness must be named or identified, then we shall have to name ourselves as it! Now you have allowed your opponent to see the result of how his game of good and bad has backfired upon him. That is, to deny him his arrogance, and his presumption of thinking he shall define himself, and to see him humiliated is a rare pleasure. Your opponent will now see that our enemy shall be allowed the honor of defining us as we defend him. This is not a simple turn the other cheek, but a straightforward invitation to write the book. For the religious in the audience of our candidate, of course the moment was ripe for an untold number of voters to see that here was a man, truly prepared to turn the course of civilization. He, in my humble opinion, should have gone for more, and even ventured to say that after our "enemy" has had the opportunity to define us, and then destroyed one half of the country, we shall offer him the other half too.

Dear Purefoy,

No, just because the national candidates did it that way does not mean they did it right, and already the price in lost votes is mounting for the mistakes of that event. In fact, some of our opponents justifiably parodied our convention for the duration. Frankly, I was finally glad to see the debacle done with, except for that crowning of the emperor thing at the end. Magnificent.

You see, when some of our people get in front of the country, they lapse in the endless discipline they must exercise. Many acted as though they were in a secluded bubble of euphoria, though the convention was an affair on exhibit to the public; therefore it should have been treated as a public affair by everyone. I even witnessed some of our "free" press rhapsodic at the speeches and clapping and genuflecting beneath our candidates and virtually indistinguishable from the rest of the swooning masses. This adds to the perception that the press is one of us: a point apparently lost to the press members in ecstasy, some with their eyes closed as if praying to the candidates or to the god who sent Them.

Whether a camera is rolling in the cave, or the condominium, or the coliseum, it is still running and therefore makes us susceptible to the judgment of an audience. You see, we do not reveal our true selves when no one is looking, because we always assume someone is looking, and therefore we are always on the watch for an audience that may be watching us. This fact was missed in the week's hooliganism. This means we must be aware of our audience ever minute we have an audience and assume we always do. I suppose some stupidly forgot that caution from the inside of the convention floor, while the whole nation is nevertheless listening to and weighing them at home. Believe you me, the atmosphere of an unruly gyrating rock concert within an arena and as seen on television by outside viewers are two different things. Thus, if there is too much swooning at the convention, or the wrong kind, a television viewer a mile away or two thousand miles away is apt to count it a farce or the behavior of buffoons. The mystic experience inside the cocoon is lost on the critter eating the morsel from the outside.

Aside from that oversight, there were also grievous slips of the tongue—or some things worded oh so carelessly. Granted, we try to marry a few contraries in our political heads, but one needs to be careful of such unions with more than a chunk of the country listening. So one of the speakers, in the same breath, indeed in the same sentence, talked about the "American Dream" of rags to riches, but then affirms that we as a nation should be outraged at the presence of rags. I would not have put those two things together as closely as did that speaker. The savvy listener can rightly—but to our detriment—deduce that we are advocating riches while trumpeting welfare. We of course care not a whit for prosperity, but instead lust for its absence.

You see, we are not advocating prosperity in the manner of our opponent, but condemning it, though not overtly, of course. We are not advocates of the "American Dream," because the moral of that dream rends our message. The rags to riches story finds the hero of the story at the end of the story. We do not. We find our man in the beginning, the stage of rags, in other words, and make sure that he sees a few of the rich, which are our villains, while he stays with his rags—poor and envious and encouraged to vote for us because of it. We do not talk to him about how he keeps himself in that condition. Thus, there are no charges from us of undisciplined living and gargantuan bills demanding money to feed voracious habits. Instead tell him someone is responsible for his woes—the rich.

The achiever of the touted "American Dream," moreover, turns a potential friend into our political foe. As I have told you constantly, we are not for the fewest people with the most, but the most people with the least. This social mobility article of faith in the "American Dream" can be used as fodder for our touting of class warfare, but it is not our dream, because at bottom we disdain it, while we prudently pay covert lip service to it. It is the dream of our opposition nevertheless. We cannot truly claim it as our own, but the country identifies with it, so we must pay homage to it. Therefore, we must find a way to use it against our political opponent and thus for us. This we do by pointing out the masses missing the dream, with the implication that we want all to realize that dream. We could actualize that dream with our dream of socialism (though not just yet, as I keep warning), in which all are equally poor, or at least as rich as the richest, which in socialism is never pronounced, and thus keeps the masses voting for us.

Of course maybe the undisciplined speaker meant that fulfillment of the "American Dream" belongs to everyone, those who dream and those who do not. I suppose that is what she maybe meant, and perhaps in the context of the pampering convention, the speaker did the best she could with her bit about the welfare necessitated for those distant from the dream.

But you see, or you should see, that there is something here that exposes our innermost viscera and cuts to the quick, and thus we need to be aware of controlling it in the presence of too many other eyes and ears. Having realized it, one must learn to live with it by controlling exposure to it. My letters must be read and studied in the light of that realization and it is this: ours is a philosophy not of government, but of grievance that overtakes government for itself. That is, to raise our grievance of lacking equality amongst all citizens, we must violate the very foundation upon which people consent to government at all. Nevertheless, our voters scarcely notice our philosophy of government as long as their kitchen table is supple enough, and we scarcely mind that they do not mind, as long as they keep us in government.

The point is that grievance can be made into a government only by encouraging an avenging jealousy which disdains the presence of inequality among citizens. Thus, we cannot seriously but only deceitfully tout any "American Dream," because any goal realized by some is never realized by all. We thus take the side of the some not, and lodge blame for those denied the dream at the feet of our opponent, while at the same time loathing a dream that creates the inequalities we hate.

The fact of the matter is that the kind of equality we desire is of a kind never found at the end, but only in the beginning. We shall therefore strive to make any finish line look precisely as the starting line, and with equal numbers, and thus by persuasion if possible, but with stronger persuaders if necessary. You know what I mean. This is why few will consent to government by our principles, and this is why grievance must be strong and vocal before we can become powerful. You see, we must necessarily work from where there is dissatisfaction, and where there is none, we must fabricate.

In short, and to revert to some archaic terminology, poverty is not the natural state of humankind, as proved by the fact that from that state, we foment most of our revolutions for a better state. However, in a country where poverty is not the order of the day, and where inequalities amongst classes are not significantly pronounced, we find our greatest challenge. We can of course deny both as facts, but better to notice that any crack of difference amongst the classes must be exploited for maximum gain of fissure, so that we can move in and become entrenched in the voting public. We must, on the other hand, never permit the observation or admission—fatal to our political connivings—that prosperity is the natural condition of humankind. Prosperity is nevertheless the host we require for the Robin Hood cleansing we will exercise on the people. Our bleating of our grievances thus becomes our entryway into political office.

If all of this is too difficult for you, do not even mention the "American Dream," in your campaign. The "disenfranchised" attracts more attention.

Dear Purefoy,

Small towns mean a small amount of votes from the small-minded. Therefore you need not bother with them when there are large cities with massive voter potential. Remember that as a man of the people you must be with the people and most importantly with the most people who have come to expect more from you than your opponent could possibly give to them. Therefore pick the cities to do your vote getting, and the larger the city the better. Those country fools, by contrast, may even tell you they don't need you, or perhaps take a gun after you. Don't worry; you don't need them either—not even for the voting booth.

As if this is not reason enough to point your feet toward the people centers in your district, remember too that our political ideas already thrive with commendable vitality among city dwellers. In fact there are some cities in these lower forty-eight where our opponents with even strenuous work can garner no more than every fourth voter. In our favorite city of the nation, indeed our beloved capitol, it is almost ninety per cent of the voters that dutifully follow us rather than our opponents.

You might ask that if the cities are givens for us, why bother with them. The reason is simple. The still-unconverted urbanities, however small their numbers, are always larger than the rural small town populations dotting our land and taking up space where cities could be built. Convert the remaining unconverted in the cities. With regard to the unconverted in the rural areas and small towns—don't bother.

Oh yes, I know, there is the thought of symbolism in carrying the votes of the rural small towns, but symbolism only carries substance if it translates into votes. What voting bloc decides on the basis of the vote of the rural voter to vote for you? The rural small town voter. So as I said, he does not have enough votes in his sparsely populated backwater for you to visit him even if you get him to vote for you, along with Jim and Joe down the potholed road they live on. Again, spend your time not with the least number of people who are the least among men, but with the most people. More is better; less is losing. Any symbolism that comes with converting the backwards voter into your voter is only meaningful for the vote you already have, and not for your urbanite who thinks urban. In fact, if your multitudes of urbanites perceive that you are popular among the rural half-civilized, they may change their vote. So stay away from the rural areas and small towns. They are not worth the trouble, and worse, they can make trouble for you.

You see, we never get many votes from these people because they are independently minded. It would well nigh take a revolution to convert them to the ways of dependency that we inculcate in our trusting voters. The rural rustics are hardly even sociable. All our talk of the group, the herd, society, and the masses is alien to people who may resist even their relative down the lane if given the chance. As some of ours have said, they live by their god and their gun. We hate both, and we tell them if they will vote for us, they will need neither of the other two. They are caught in a time warp and exist as children in adult bodies. Best to let them be. Their numbers don't matter and they matter less every election as there are less of them with every turn of the calendar. Neither secularization nor socialization nor socialism have caught up to them, and so there is little chance for you to reach them, unless their wallets start to shrink when the economy sours. Moreover, you know that when economies turn bad, people migrate not from the city to the country, but to the colossal collective that we call the city. Here there will at least be a bread line or a shelter of some sort. The rural ruffian's introduction to the city is their introduction to the fact that we can help even their kind when times are rough. Let a bad economy convert these rustic rebels for you. When they show up in the city they will in time convert themselves to you.

But in the meantime, one must toss bones to venerated objects, however unworthy of affection such things actually are. This occasional but necessary deference to our rural brethren is one such cumbersome necessity, though rather like the venerated "American Dream." So, therefore, you will need on occasion to show some modicum of respect toward this uncouth group of our population who we privately despise because they are furthest removed from us, both by miles and medullas. Like attracts like, and so we are not attracted to each other. That being said, you can nevertheless toss in a cliché every now and then about the great American "pioneering spirit," still alive out on the prairies, or the Alaskan tundra, or held up with loaded gun in the mountain hovels. If you easily fatigue over this nonsense about frontier and pioneers—and indeed you will some of the time—then find a way to use it to preach your message, and some of their young, anxious to escape the morbidness of the rural small towns, will be pulled into our cities and begin to vote for us.

It is easy to do, and one hardly need wait for shrinking wallets and a bad economy. Simply point out the mammoth differences between life in the backwoods and life in the high-rise. Start by talking about rural poverty, for example. Most of the young of the rural barbarians can be drawn away to the dream of the city by indicating just how rough life is when eked out on the creek bank. They may have never noticed their plight until you tell them, but of course with media spinning another world into every crevice these days, the sod busters and all their kind can see and hear it all on their electronic gadgetry from the barn or the cellar or the swamp. Even the rural folk of just a generation or two ago had trouble keeping their youngsters down on the farm, but with all the media showing the glitz of city life, fewer and fewer of the young can resist the temptation of escape from their wretched rural existence.

Of course, some of our misguided strategists imagine that such peculiar populations as you encounter in our backwaters demand populist politicians. These strategists presume that we must make ourselves into the image of the ignorant in order to draw the vote of these rural ruffians who identify more with their general store than the storehouse that is our capital. We are all for populism when it makes us electable, but populism of the old kind went out with log cabins and tobacco. We despise both. To be a populist today requires you to be a man of the people, but remember where the most people live. Nor does populism today mean coarseness; it means "main-stream," as we call it. This of itself is enough to keep you away from the wrong worry of thinking these country people are worth any political effort. Of course, we are no more mainstream than they—those of our political persuasion are about as far from the main stream as the Volga is from the Potomac—but the point to grasp for vote getting is that populism today is not guns and tobacco and bibles. Do not therefore show sympathy or support for this kind of culture of ignorance masking itself as the best citizens in waiting for a proper candidate. While one cannot precisely show open disdain for our backwater cultures, one should try to ignore them. When the ugly voice from such parts is raised and becomes strident with its trademark victorianism and godism and gunism, let your voters know that you will have nothing to do with the fringe elements of our country. You can even tout that you had rather lose the election than be ushered into office by the votes of such people. Remember, they have very few votes compared to the bounty of our teeming cities. So go ahead and say that you had rather lose your election than have the votes of rascals, for then you can reap your reward: you will be honored as one politician still standing up for principle, and you will be counted a man of inscrutable moral courage. Once the applause is over after such an announcement by you, you can absent yourself from the deafening applause in a back room for a minute, and with some of your staff have the laugh of your life over the fools making your political career possible.

Remember, and I have failed to say it for a while, but do not forget: your political quest is all sliding board if done rightly. I mean correctly. Don't make this journey to your political office harder than it needs to be. Look for the crowds. In our country you don't even have to make them. They are already made. They are called cities. Stay away from any other place. Do not leave the ninety and nine to go for a mere one.

Dear Purefoy,

Of course you can benefit from all the talk about going "green" these days! The bounty of this issue alone is enough to assure you victory, if handled correctly. Handle it correctly and in a timely manner, because the election is just around the corner. But first I must instruct you in how to deal with your "popular" opponent and quickly, since by the tone of your letter it seems that even you may vote for her. You should have noticed that your opponent is not green, though according to research submitted to me, she comes from the rural barrenness of wide open nothingness. The rural rustics do not romanticize their environment because they know the difficulties of prying out a living from it, and thus are rarely zealously green; our urban voters, who vastly outnumber them, loathe their own lack of greenery and are therefore romanticizing green idiots who vote for us. Must I tell you yet again to go with the most voters?

You have to have one thing uppermost in your mind about this election: to win it. Therefore, what it takes to win is what you must do within the provisions of law, but also without if circumstances permit. The candidate you are running against is of course important, but still ultimately beside the point of winning; the point is to win no matter who the opponent. Given the goal of winning, adjustments may become necessary because of the variables any opponent presents: none, however formidable or intimidating they may seem, are insurmountable. Even if God were running as the opposition candidate, we would still present opposition to that candidate and furthermore, expect to win.

Normally, capitalize on the weaknesses of your opponent, and if she has none—though of course she does, which therefore means you have not yet found them—invent some, and sell them to the public. If the list of her failures fails to turn her voters into your voters, then you have miserably failed to show her weaknesses sufficiently to unseat her popularity with the public; therefore invent stronger charges against her. If someone does not choke at the table from the spoonful of food provided, obviously you need to increase the quantity for the desired effect. And remember, small untruths scarcely turn an ear anymore; you must go for the big stuff. Voters don't hear the miniscule these days. Mere infidelity will not do—not being sufficiently green will do. In our business you cannot think small. Thinking on that order will give you a small amount of votes on Election Day, and you can go back to bed with a tranquilizer instead of a big office with celebratory champagne.

Because you need to put more into an ear these days to turn it, you must carefully ratchet up your criticism of any opponent. Make it of significant size for catastrophic effect. If you merely but incessantly criticize her with tissue paper complaints, she and her adoring public will grow tired of listening to such droning and they will sense that you fear her by not being able to leave her alone. If she is constantly tagged in your speeches, and yet you have nothing significantly damaging on her, your criticism of her will damage you. Therefore, criticize her very infrequently, but when you do, introduce a load of devastating information on her, and then go back to your own political platform of everything for most every voter except the rich. Our free press will now pick up your charges and complete the damage to your opponent for you without costs.

Nevertheless, even though the press at large is in league with us, we can hardly expect them to do all of our digging for us, (though of course there are constant offers) for then they shall be caught on our side of the fence. Thus you need to take our press to the site where you found the dirt. There the grave for your opponent's political aspirations can be prepared for you by them. The job of the press, which they will of course relish, will be to dig the hole even deeper for your opponent for her defeat and thus your victory. Such an exchange manifests the exquisite nature of the symbiotic relationship our candidates have with the press and the press with us. One day, of course, we will come out and make it all legal by marrying. Now we are only too glad to use the whore that prostitutes herself for us: a willing accomplice who even offers to do our pleasure when we do not ask.

For the bombshell needed to attract sufficient voter attention some research is needed. That is, you must have your people digging in the dirt round the clock until something so significant is found so as to turn the voting upside down in your favor. If you cannot find anything damaging enough to enable our partner press to pounce on our joint opponent, you have only one recourse left. You will have to take the only route open to you.

You must sell your voting public on the belief that no commoner can run a government as complex as we have made it. It is only simpletons who want to make government simpler. Therefore no brawn nor bravery nor brunette can take the place of the required specialist to run colossal government. The common sense of commoners therefore comes to nonsense when applied to the complexities of high office. Undoubtedly, a candidate who resonates with the ignorant public will be ignorant like the people who like them. You must therefore show the public just how ignorant their darling candidate is, without intimating too strongly that followers have the vices of those they follow.

As I said some time ago, you do not need the ignorant rural and small town voters, but more to the point and more importantly, you must convince your voters that the country does not need candidates that come from such parts either. The possibility of a country hack running government is indeed terrifying, because it presents us with the scenario that a mere rural small town publican could end up as a head of state. You must therefore portray her viciously: as something of a Pharisee, or better a puritan to start with, with all the dark and dank images such a word connotes.

No commoner must be allowed to scale any such heights as that required for the work of government; commoners must be kept down on the farm with their animals for company they can keep. The election of one of their kind would serve as the severest rebuke to professional politicians of our sort and would constitute a sort of takeover of the farm by the animals. Worse, a country bumpkin would be running our country—our country, a modern, secular, and urban country conversant more with civilization than fields, but now put in jeopardy by someone who trucks more with rain and hay and harvest and fishing and seasons than diplomacy. This is why you must pollute the assumed purity of such a candidate not just by dirt, but for thinking they can run such an office as ours. Only professionals can do what we do; the Jeffersonian idea adored by some of our own was wrong. Keep these rural and small town know-nothings away from political office.

Dear Purefoy.

Yes, we must exercise caution in our handling of the financial crisis; we can package it for our gain, but prudence is required before we can do our plucking. If we spea[illegible] of the crisis in a manner that avoids faulting our policie[illegible] [illegible]his current unpleasantness, we can continue not just [illegible] come out ahead—that means at the ballot box. In[illegible] live high off the hog too. Why have you not invi[illegible] drink you owe after your last whining correspon[illegible]

The fact of the matter—which we can with ease hide from view by saying opposite things to our voting public—is that much if not well nigh this entire financial tremor occurs under the weight of our recklessness with money, which our minions advanced legislatively. This means that on occasion we get squeezed for having dispensed more money than this wretched and selfish capitalist economy will allow the poor to have. Of our charitable legislative effort to provide homes to the homeless—by opting out of an economy that loves dollars more than humans—we now witness a theft of our generosity by men of the opposition who love mammon more than men. The check of charity we extended to the needy is eventually shredded in the demand for more dollars than people on charity have. This is to say that our politics and capitalism are ill poised to work together, and we know which one has to go. So too our opponents and not us. Now is the time to trumpet that call, again, but with considerably more bravado as election time draws exquisitely close. The people without the dollars, to whom we have extended our charity with our dollars, see that they have not been given enough dollars to survive a hungry creditor. They are without a house and a home, again. They are your voters in waiting—for you! The insatiable hunger of voracious creditors demanding people live in the world of capitalist money has bankrupted these borrowers. Cast all the blame on the greed of the greedy, saving none of the blame for us and surely none for the grieving borrowers. We need not even go for the voter in such a time, for they will flock to us like sheep for the bounty we have to offer. Be ready.

We of course need not in the least look bad in any of this. In other words, we can simply continue bleating our mantras about the greediness of the rich continuing to milk the country until the rich have it all and the poor have even less than nothing. In different words, we can simply, though without using the word, sing praises to our socialist humanism by projecting this financial tremor as brought about not by us, but by people who care nothing for people in their greater love for money. We have laid down our money for our sheep, but now -apitalist wolf has again demanded more payment than we generous shepherds have extended to those weakened by poor credit. Therefore, the homeless should have been given even more cash than their poor credit allowed. The rich have simply tried to shake the trousers of the borrower empty by shaking too hard—for every last cent until they kill the flailed body. All our standard talking points are undented by this unpleasant financial meltdown, because we will make it the responsibility of our political opposition. They are about money, money, money; we are about people, people, and people. We raise people up; they raze people down. The people are now down; therefore our opponents are responsible for them being down and our voters looking done in by the whole affair. We shall raise them up.

Therefore, the current tremors are building blocks for us and the socialist house we must now move forward, amidst this havoc wrought by the capitalists among us. Remember what I have said, our times are the best in the worst of times. Grievance is our gateway into government; nobody in good health, financial or otherwise, will visit, much less call upon our social planners, on a sunny day. We simply wait for the rainy day, or the tsunami, or the earthquake, or the drought, or the hurricane, or the blessing of financial unease. Our "help" in waiting now has takers created by the want ensuing from such calamities as we cherish. Prudence can portend plenty for you if you can manipulate the want of the peoples to satisfy your want—political office. It is not difficult, though caution is necessary. It is all sliding board when done correctly, even when it looks as if the world is shaking forever downward around you, for our traction is best when the earth is shaking. The shaking gives us opportunity to shift the country toward us. So you can privately applaud every catastrophe known to humans, because then the opportunity for our nanny state gets some legs and then some arms and then a trunk, which will eventually give it some teeth. This will not be noticed, but better yet, not even objected to, for we will offer a world of caring underneath the soft word of compassion. In a brutal world that buries its dead as paupers because they are paupers and have been made paupers by their creditors—the capitalists—we will be welcomed as life savers.

When reality hits hardest, we have it easiest. We work when the world is down; the world takes no account of us when it is up. Therefore, when it is up, we must bring it down. This we just did—read my first paragraph again—but we can assign responsibility for it to our opponent and few will think anything to the contrary. Certainly not our adoring press, which is just as happy about this seismic shift for us as we are happy for them. Look at the polls—they are looking up.

Of course people will be flocking to their gods in such tumultuous times, but your job is to show them that we are all they need. This is why we detest other gods; they take from us the respect and allegiance which belongs only to us. Also, the other religious are always trying to take the government away from us by taking it upon themselves with their fiendish faith-based outsourcing. We cannot allow any of it, and what we most cannot allow is any indication of success on the part of our competitors. This we do by refusing to acknowledge consequences, either their good ones or our failures. Intent is our hallowed and sanctifying icon: by it many a scurrilous program has been propped up and exalted even when living in the trash heap of failure.

Yes, extraordinary opportunity is knocking at our door. The country most known in the modern world for bulging prosperity has been humbled and rebuked. Our chance extends beyond this current election, moreover, as we go about showing the voters that the market economy in time always implodes upon its citizens. Father Marx taught us it was inevitable and our victory unstoppable, but even some of our own had started to doubt of late, especially after our brethren to the east saw their socialist paradise fall to ruin some time ago. But just as Rome was not made in a day, nor will it fall in a day. So too our situation now. Be patient, but poised and prepared to act.

Many of the brethren thought our cause in the throes of death for the past couple decades, but out of the ashes we can rise again if we play this current crisis for our gain. Therefore, tell your voters, and then tell them again and loudly, that the money mongers created this mess, and that, in the spirit of love, we shall provide for their material plenty that the money mongers stole for themselves. Out of this crisis it will become obvious for all to see what political ideology should be running the country. Help them to see it.

Dear Purefoy,

Yes, the youth vote is more important than any sector of our voter base. It is the most assured block of voters we have and so must accordingly be guarded against defections and any dubious infiltrations by our opponents. Those young people between the ages of 18 and about 23 are a gold mine for us, because this group is virtually exempt from tax responsibility so we can tout all our lavish and budget-busting programs, and the harangue of opponents about costs will mean little to nothing for voters who have scarcely paid for anything yet, beyond a large cup of coffee. Better yet, some colleges of late do not even charge for that; it is all a matter of "social justice" they say: let him who is thirsty drink. The old fogey notion of justice as something extracted from people is receding; we have turned it around to mean something that keeps on giving. That aside, such experience serves to indoctrinate our youth with the notion that everything should cost nothing and can because mother government is picking up the tab. These students may have loans for their education that force them to notice the real world a bit, but the idea of money due rarely sinks in until actual payments come from their wallets, usually after graduation. At this point we may start to lose a few of them as faithful voters—when they must start to pay for the previous plenty—but the way to keep them voting for us is to preach to them their right to an education, which of course means paid for by our beloved government. If no education bills are due after their graduation, thanks to us and another gift of social justice, then they are just as apt to vote for us as before. Then they will be ready for the next gift from us: sub-prime mortgages, etc.

These young people tend to have few fixed points of reference, so we can lead them astray as we wish, for no elastic band will pull them back from whence they came, because they are prepared to stray from any base camp if enticed sufficiently. Once they see our camp, moreover, their days of wandering are over as they become settled into our world, with little desire to make inquiry about any other. Who, for example, can resist the temptation of a free this and a free that, and all the talk about living in a more humane world grounded in compassion and cooperation and justice rather than competition and conflict and injustice? They will think they have found heaven without the painfully inconvenient event of dying. And they will: our heaven on mother earth they can occupy and all we ask for in return—not their money, someone else's will do just fine—but their vote! We offer them an experiment in politics that sounds as utopian as many youth inevitably tend to be, so they go with us, and not with our heartless and crusty opponents—still monotonously preaching their stodgy message of personal "responsibility." We of course do not want to convert too many of this hostile group, so as to lessen their numbers too substantially, because they supply the necessary financing for our social experiments. We therefore need an enemy such as they because they serve our purposes—or our purse—if you will. As long as we can continue to steal from them with at least a façade of legality about it, we will continue to do so.

We are further helped by the sort of education our youthful voter can count on these days in most of the colleges. In fact, at such colleges education is hardly to be called an education in the old sense of the word, because our fine institutions are for the most part doing a darling job of indoctrinating the youth with our politics, even in some cases without the mask or pretence of actual learning, and so when they come out they are prepared to vote for us, with few questions asked. In fact, the universities are largely absent of irksome questions these days, for our teachers are prepared to give them the answers without the questions, and most students are prepared to take what they are given, especially when they see the benefits that correct answers offer to the chosen individuals. Some—the best—even come away ignorant of the realization that there are any questions at all about the answers we supply from our lecterns.

This change in schooling culture from love of knowledge to the demand for obedience has come about because the rabble rousers of old have become the wardens of the new schoolhouse, and with this formidable regime in place little rabble rousing is tolerated anymore. In other words, we are firmly in command of the votes of the youth, because we are in command of the education of our youth. They know what they are told to know, and they have too little experience of the world to know otherwise. They are as prepared to serve us as the accommodating press, which, by the way, we encourage our brighter youth to enter and thus further contribute to our worthy cause. Though not to belabor this point, remember what our Master taught us: that the point is not to understand the world but to change it. If the Man who could write for the highest degree of the university could see that, then surely we can get others who can barely write—both inside and outside our educational institutions—to glimpse it. Our educational establishments and their protected and pampered professors are to be commended for their superb work. "Carry on," we say to them and their marvelous products: our voters.

Because of this agreeable situation, scarcely any heavy exertion is needed to assure that this effortless slice of the voter pie fall our way, for its members are virtually guaranteed to do in the voting booth what we want done and, furthermore, to scarcely think about what they are doing as they are doing it. Remember what I told you in the beginning. The problem in our business is boredom because we have so much wrapped up and packaged for us already. By having the formula for success at the ballot box revealed to you, by me, political success is yours. Now is no time to doze, however, with the election looming large and immediately in front of us. The Sky is Falling speech is always good to attract a few more recalcitrant voters and always a good stir. If they don't fall for that, tell them it has already fallen, and our opponents have blinded them to that fact. My favorite is the Cosmic speech, in which we vilify our opponent as from the infernal regions and ourselves as a kind of Prometheus who steals fire from heaven for the benefit of earth. (Prometheus was, by the way, the mythological character most esteemed by the Master, and thus it is not unbefitting that some among our number count the esteemed Lucifer the best model for our purposes.)

We have for you smeared your opponent into the dirt from whence she imagines she came, rather than from our true primate ancestors, but you still cannot ignore her completely, nor assume she will be silent or subdued for long. The ignorant are always prone to speak out of the turn we allow them. Furthermore, these religious quacks are frequently resilient beyond prediction, so expect the unexpected from her. Though she has the look of youthful promise about her, you must persuade your voters that her political and social ideas belong to the gray-headed and past centuries and not to any current mainstream of thought. Certainly she has nothing to offer our youth but the menacing prison of that vaunted institution of the "family" that we have broken down for some decades now, and that "life" nonsense that permits her to bring anything into the world under the delusion that her imagined god loves it too. Furthermore, she has no education we would recognize in our schools, and thus she must be seen as the outsider she is. Her adorers look upon her as someone formidable; we must continue to portray her as a freak.

Dear Purefoy,

We don't have any principles to compromise, except our commitment to winning elections, and that is never compromised. It is never subjected to doubt or scrutiny by us, even from a distance, no matter what the state of the world or of ourselves. In short, winning is first on our list; everything else is second and beyond. As one from the gridiron used to say, "winning is not everything, it is the only thing." Moreover, everything else is background to the stage set for defeating our opponents. This gives our effort at election singular focus and keeps us steadily on track because we know our unquestioned goal is never to suffer a detour. Therefore, you can quit your recurring worries, again, over eliciting voters whose only worth to us is that they vote for us. The fact that we use them to further our own ends—election to office—presents no rumbling of conscience for us, because we don't have one to worry with: neither should you. The votes of our voters are our reason for concern for them.

Your question about religious voters is a pertinent one in a country still dripping with religion. Such voters are sometimes the key to elections won and lost; therefore, we must have them within our sights, particularly in these last days of campaigning, and more importantly, you must know how to lure them into the voting booth with us, in good conscience. They do present onerous obstacles at times, but also great opportunity if handled with sufficient skill. So that you end up a recipient of the latter, listen carefully.

The religious are obsessed with their archaic notions of right and wrong, saint and sinner, that most of the enlightened abandoned light years ago. We believe in no such obsolescence or pedantry, but we do have a hook with the religious voter despite our disbelieving depravity. The similarity between us and them some will notice even without our pointing. To even the lesser-witted intellects among them, we curiously resemble them in their clamoring cry for forgiveness simply because we oftentimes "let bygones be bygones." We, in other words, are willing to let trespasses go unnoticed. We do in fact encourage this trait in others—if to our benefit and gain, i.e., votes—and tout it from the rooftops if it offers advantage to one among our numbers who may have fallen. Ultimately, however, we feign this "forgiveness" nonsense over wrongdoing because we take no offense at "sin." Nevertheless, the religious among our voters may surmise that we irreligious are religious without knowing it: thus they view us as possibly tolerable. If they reason a bit more, they may surmise that this presumed similarity between us and them is because their religion, though rejected by modern secular people, nevertheless shows a residual effect even among the mockers and debauchers—ourselves. Thus, for example, and aside from the whole "forgiveness" quaintness, we seculars still clamor and demand and believe that the oppressed will eventually triumph over the oppressor, as our Master inexorably believed and taught us to believe. Some of our own scholars give some dubious credence to this mistaken relationship, as if we secularists are unable to resist the Christian and religious message steeped in our bones: though shed it we have from our skins. This, of course, is all nonsense, but tolerable nonsense, for if our religious voters apprise us in such a manner that causes them to vote for us—then we applaud their mistaken thinking.

It is nevertheless a mistake for us to see ourselves connected to any religion in this way, however; furthermore, we have no patience for those among us hankering backwards to darkness by reconverting back to whence they came by this pseudo-resemblance of light to darkness. We are indebted to no one nor to any belief for our actions, except our own. The Master himself would disown any such religious pollution, or more to the point, outright thievery, of his true theory. As he so eloquently wrote, what happens happens because it happens. There is no "ought" attempting to right an upside-down world. The Master saw clearly the direction and cycles of history and simply pointed out that what will be will be. Thus, we have history on our side; god and fairies will have to be relegated to the fantasies claiming fatuous responsibility for the socialist march of history. We do accept converts, however, but from where they come and how they come, we care not a bit. Tell your religious voter that if he is troubled on his journey to us, that what he must do—in language that he can understand—is to be born again, because his prior rebirth was the wrong one.

Excuse the diversion, except if you win this election you will have to school yourself in the theory after you have benefitted from the practice of our politics. The Master will perhaps forgive our interest in the theory after he cautioned that our point is not to understand the world but convulse it.

So, the religious among your voters may take your leniency toward wrongdoing, their "sin," as an earmark of "grace," albeit this concept is as much of a stranger to us as the antiquated "sin" notion. Hopefully what the religious voter drawn to you will not notice is that you are as dismissive of grace as you are of sin; the fact that you go past human foibles with such indifference is because you have indifference to these bogus religious unrealities of “sin” and “grace.” To your advantage, nevertheless, is the fact that your curious religious voter may think you exceed him in your readiness to extend “grace” to the wrongdoer. He has thus completely misread your action, but all to your benefit—his vote!! Your retraction of judgment in the face of wrongdoing shames his sinful propensity to judge; you, therefore, have trumped him in the practice of his “grace,” even as you are on a clear day, distinctly and thus noticeably anti-religious. His head will now spin, but his pencil is also being prepared to put a check by your name on the ballot. He will rack it up to his mysterious god; we care not from where his vote comes, as long as it comes. We in consequence will be elected because this potential voter in his stupidity mistakes us as one of his own. Even this revelation he may not fret over, but rather, and better, count himself more broadminded than his brethren who cannot imagine a wolf having a place in the sheepfold, whereas he, now enlightened, can. In fact, if he keeps it up, he may even consider that what he thought of as sheep are indeed goats, and what he thought of as goats are indeed sheep. Your goal by the next election cycle is to see him replace his whole outdated tyrannical religion with ours. Probably, however, you will have nothing to do for him, because he will do it all for himself. All sliding board, again. Meanwhile, we will, with help such as this, turn the world upside down.

Dear Purefoy,

Yes, I think our beloved socialism is making inroads by leaps and bounds within our country in these days of seismic swings and downturns of the financial sectors, particularly the stock market. Remember what I said earlier: we get our best traction when the ground is shaking, and it hardly gets better than an excruciating financial earthquake that portends a meltdown. The Master told us last century that it was inevitable. Those who had little faith some years ago when the ugly capitalism pronounced itself the winner of the world are suffering a rebuke today they could never imagine then. The faithful stood unmoved but tenured and ready. The faithful, moreover, never wavered and are now seeing their long-awaited reality come to fruition. Workers of the world unite, you have everything to gain and so many to punish.

Our opponent's camp is in disarray, much to our and your advantage. Furthermore, the state of this financial peril is world-wide, and our European brethren are looking very favorably upon using this occasion for the backwater America to come into the socialist mainstream with them at long last. Our prior dissenting voice against the inhuman free market economy is now in the ascendency in our land, and we shall thus be able in time, in collusion with our European brethren, to position ourselves from a perch of unassailability. No beatific vision could be as beautiful as this.

Our incumbent opposition is in a well nigh impossible position from which to save any of their ideology. Better, they seem perfectly prepared to abandon much of it. This financial trembling is happening on their watch, and as we observe them, they seem oddly accommodating toward laying the new platform of socialism on top of the capitalist rot on their freefall way out of office. This is a puzzle, of course; but enemies are not always to be understood, though they are always your enemy. I can only possibly explain such a move as naïve shock that the failure of their darling market economics leaves them speechless. Once again, sometimes one would wish for an opponent with a little more fight so that we do not die of boredom. It is as if they simply and silently hand us the victory baton for our turn.

Our opponents seem afraid to pin any tails on the responsible donkey for this crisis. Indeed, the mystery is that they seem to know the culprits; in fact, they have mentioned a name or two when called upon to do so after a supporter demands it of them, but they try to remain evermore the "gentlemen" for us to defeat. If I were in charge of them, I would tell one and all that there is no victory of any kind in defeat; they seem to think there is some kind of honor in losing. Their mistake here is to have underestimated their opponents—us. Thus, they continuously talk about being "bipartisan," and apparently mean it, with no realization that this position when made to work for us is only a temporary accommodation before the amassing and holding of all power. We therefore welcome such talk by our opponents, in fact encourage it, and all the while know from our experience with our opponents, that they do not regard this "bipartisan" nonsense as a simple subterfuge of expedience as we do.

They surprisingly seem to have little knowledge of economics—this may account for our opposition being virtually silent on the socialism advancing more and more every hour. More compromising to their politics, however, is that they seem to think that they can match the amount of money we are prepared to reroute from one taxpayer to another nonpayer to relieve this financial crisis. As I have said to you repeatedly, when our opponents start to mimic our message or our actions, you can bet that in their minds they think they are losing. They nevertheless start to ape us: to play piggyback. In this situation, however, the truth of the matter may be even better than that for us. In other words, our opponents may be even more ignorant than we could imagine. That is, they may only clumsily notice any kind of difference between a free-market economy and our aspiring socialism. Of course, you have economists that align themselves with our opponents and that notice the welcoming mat for socialism in this meltdown, but they cannot get their candidates to demarcate any real difference between their solution and ours as it concerns staving off further financial turmoil. On the other hand, they may know the difference, but in their self-defeating sense of bipartisanship refrain from drawing any attention to it. So they are either ignorant or naively bipartisan, or both. Either one or both work to our advantage.

If these opponents are not too much of a worry for us anymore, the economists I just spoke of do present a bit of an obstacle. Thus we have our academic minions and press out in mass against the free marketers. These free market economists have now picked up the fact that non-credit-worthy mortgages were too much for their darling free market to digest, so after a while it throws them up and out, precipitating in particular a quandary for the banking industry or others who ended up holding such mortgages. Thus, the devotees of the free market contend that the government pressure which urged and cajoled and intimated lenders into backing such mortgages, applied pressures their vaunted market could not bear.

All the free marketers clamor for freedom as if it were divine; none ask if the ordinary citizen should have a freedom from fear, as that right was articulated by one of our most articulate spokesmen decades ago. Voters left with a house they cannot pay for are in the grip of fear right now: their home repossessed or on the docket for repossession. We have a golden political opportunity to counter the apologists for an inhumane market that jerks people from their bed and their kitchen table to throw them on the street. The market apologists deify and respect every spike and drip of the market and ignore the people the market throws on the street. Time for that market to go and people to move back into their houses. Thank goodness that even our opponents are closer to us than these rank free-marketers. As I told you in the very beginning, we are on the verge of having one political point of view in this country, and these economists spoken of here excepted, the attempts of most all the current politicians to address the financial trauma of late confirms this. We are on the edge of a possible socialist millennium.

Dear Purefoy,

Yes, your lead is expanding over your opponent, and so now, for the most part, you can start to ignore him. (I am speaking of your opponent as generic, for reasons that will become evident in this letter.) This simply means you start to talk about implementing your vision for the people and drop him from the picture. And do not fear all the claptrap and resentment that will come from your opponent's campaign about you assuming that you are going to be victorious, because this is precisely the image you want to project of yourself. That is, even as you continue to campaign, you really no longer have to look the part of the fretful campaigner anymore, but rather you should reflect the office holder putting the last touches on his plans for his stint as servant of the people. Therefore, except for some unlikely and highly unusual happening, you should make a point to make no more references to your opponent in any of your speeches to the voting public. After the voters see you presenting yourself as the occupant of the office you are running for—though you will scarcely look like you are running anymore, but instead occupying the office—they will assume it too.

Furthermore, to posture yourself in this matter will show great confidence on your part. Meanwhile your opponent, because you are now assuming he is no longer a factor, will have to work in the opposite direction with his own strategy. He will therefore have no time to talk about his plans or policies because he will be reminding voters that the campaign is still going, because you are creating the opposite appearance—and thus the reality—that the campaign is truly over. Your opponent knows, therefore, that the campaign being over in this way means he will lose, so he has to dislodge you from your widening lead, and the only way for him to fight that uphill battle is to attack you relentlessly. Meanwhile, you respond to nothing in his attacks within reason. This will convey to the voter that you are so assured of winning that you can neglect the most vicious attacks upon you, simply because they are irrelevant to a candidate who is going to win. Even those last words are too weak; you have won.

Thus, while you may never speak of him again in the remainder of the campaign, his campaign can speak of nothing but you in a frantic attempt to dislodge your victory or, at a minimum, to slow down your ever widening lead. His arrows will be ineffectual and his doom soon thereafter will become apparent, even to him. He will try to save some face, but only with the grossest futility. Very soon thereafter he will start to talk about his victory in his defeat, but this is the futile meander of trying to avoid the inevitable shame that comes with defeat—his defeat. It is the spurious talk of a corpse trying to retain some composure after it is dead. And from your perspective, your opponent will be dead, politically. Therefore, if the situation calls for any mention of him on your part at this point, speak respectively, as one would of the dead. He is no longer a live candidate who threatens you in any way, so show no fear of him, however desperate his gasping measures to pump some air back into himself. He is of the past, you are of the future. Tell him, in private of course, to rest in peace. He will be apt to not even spend the last few days of his campaign campaigning, but probably endure his agony in his bed, hoping to forget his miserable venture.

Meanwhile, as your race now nears an end, you may nervously be tempted to fear your comfortable reserve with reference to your opponent. However, your confidence in not even mentioning him will be sufficient inducement for him to curl up and defeat himself. Remember my first letter to you. Our job is easy, but sometimes it is even better than that, and this last stretch of your well-advised campaign is one example as you head into the backstretch; you do not even have to do anything, and yet your work gets done. In what other line of work is so little effort rewarded with so much benefit?

You must keep your rearguard on standby, however, and be ever watchful of your opponent, while you of course present the impression that you have now forgotten that at one time you ever had an opponent. Your rearguard watches for any sort of spike anywhere which would indicate some kind of ripple among voters, which could in the realm of possibility take away by inches or feet your current and comfortable lead. Thus you need to have a plan for this just in case the drowning man finds an iceberg to latch onto en route to a political recovery from the doom at the end of his losing campaign.

All that aside, and with your minions watching all your flanks, now you can turn to talking about nothing but the euphoria that will greet your voters upon your election. However, do not even refer to the "election," because all of your speeches henceforth should appear as given by one already in office. Thus, you can speak of the new world about to be, that you, in collusion with others of our political persuasion, are about to bring to fruition.

Tell the people that you and they will be wiping every tear away, and that in sufficient time, they will not remember the last occasion when life presented them with any difficulty or sadness at all. Tables will be bountiful with food; houses repossessed by unscrupulous money-loving creditors will be given back to their rightful owners; weapons will be melted down into plowshares, and even the plows will be softened so as to place no undue stress upon Mother Earth from above; law enforcement will have to find other employment of community building of some type, for the "criminal" element of society will vanish; the military will vanish too, for our "foreign enemies" will become our international friends, and our last cry will be the one whereby our voters realize that they could have had this world much sooner than today, if they had only listened to us before. We will let bygones be bygones, however, with the assurance given to them, that we will never leave them nor forsake them, now that they have placed us into power.

Dear Purefoy,

Yes, your opponent is tempting you to come out in the open to take the slugs he is firing at you. There is, of course, no absolutely correct answer that will address every occasion like this, so I will offer a general plan based on different contingencies.

If your opponent is simply offering more and more criticism of you, of uneven value, or shouting his criticisms to the rooftops with a shrill and shrieking tone of voice, that in general is an indication of his desperation. That is, if the loudness or absurdity of his attacks significantly increase, he is simply aiming his bullets wildly with the nervous hope that one will miraculously find you. An attack that takes this form you can generally ignore. You will also find that the voters in general will ignore barrage attacks like this, and the longer your opponent continues this sort of unfocused and relentless attack, the more the voters will grow impatient with him to the point of making it virtually impossible that he could be elected at all.

This posture on his part, and voter response to it, will generally be sufficient to diminish his following and bolster the size of your voting bloc. Therefore you simply need do nothing but let him grow hoarse and exhausted from his increased bellowing at you. While he continues to shout and harangue you, you can peacefully compose your victory speech. Meanwhile, the number of previously undecided voters for you escalates.

The other possibility is that one of his bullets is perceived by a significant number of your potential voters to have hit its mark. This situation is of course serious, because now one must think out a calculated response to an attack that appears to have some credibility—at least to your potential voters. Remember what I wrote to you some time ago; it matters more who people think you are, rather than what you are. Perceptions, therefore, are more important than realities on this point.

Some of our national people run into this situation of late in their campaign. A testy reporter quoted a text from Father Marx and asked how we differed. I fear our cohorts floundered a bit in their contention that the question was poisoned and therefore not worthy of an answer. To some voters, of course, the implication of refusing to answer a question is that the question may be too close for comfort. This is indeed a dangerous situation, so to avert the implication of guilt the question should have been answered. Because it still to date has not been answered by that campaign, there is considerable fidgeting and uncertainty seeping through our national campaign—in fact, the question is now finding numerous other forms and venues from our opponents. A bullet that has hit its mark cannot be ignored; it will fester the flesh if left unattended.

Our people should have put as much distance as they could between themselves and Father Marx in a country that historically has put to trial and publicly humiliated His American disciples. In fact, and to avoid anything like that, it is not out of the question that our candidates could have conceivably claimed to be completely ignorant of the name of Marx or any of His writings. One might contend that their expertise was in the Constitution of our own country, and not in the dusty works of some German vagabond. In this way, they turn the possible criticism of themselves back onto safer ground and intimate that their knowledge has been of things American, not political philosophies more akin to a river of blood.

Such an answer would have proved entirely satisfactory to the vast majority of voters and would have laid to rest at least for the time the import of the original question. However, an answer appropriate for one time and occasion may be entirely inappropriate for a different one. This is certainly the case here. By this I simply mean that the aforementioned response is conceived to throw off the hunting dogs; when we are put in charge of the dogs we can give an entirely different kind of answer—and one that is more pleasing to our Father.

This means that when we are firmly in command of the offices we aspire to now—but will occupy later—and when this question comes up again, as it will, we can simply ask what is wrong with the precept of our Father that from each according to his ability and to each according to his need should be our societal goal? So at that time, instead of disowning the precept, as formerly we would need to do, we can then defend it. By then we will have moved from defense to offense. And from campaign to office.

As momentous as a political revolution like this may seem in a country like ours—which has lived to this point in a livid horror of all things named socialist—we will have to remind ourselves that we brought it about by a bloodless event at the ballot box. Also, no voters were forced to vote for our candidates; rather, the voters did vote for us because we have prepared them over the past decades to accept of their own free will our tempting platter of government for the people by the socialists. It was a mistake of some of our predecessors from decades ago to think that our politics could only be advanced by the sword. They never dreamed that advancement could come quicker in cultures taught by us to loathe the sword.

Dear Purefoy,

Thank you for your note, and I am glad that you enjoyed yourself at the festivities on election night. The results of your campaign did not surprise me in the least. You had, after all, some superb advice. Recall what I said in my first correspondence with you about keeping these letters for your reelection bid next time.

We are, of course, standing on a historical threshold in the history of this nation, and though our time has been of long duration in coming, we shall not be disappointed now that it is here. The trauma of history is its snail's pace, but occasionally it gallops, and more is changed in the twinkling of an eye than many a millennia. Of course we shall not know for some weeks how much of our agenda we can reasonably expect to achieve, but if the past weeks are any indication I expect nothing less than our wildest dreams to come to pass. The election results confirm a shift in the political culture of the nation, and with the inches we have been given, we will be prepared to take our miles. Truly historic.

Now is our time to consolidate our gains and for you to take account of why you were victorious. We need our voters of course, but only for as long as their votes are needed. The vote, moreover, is more important than the voter; and if we can get a vote without a voter, we will always take it. The fact of the matter is that voters are fickle, and a further fact is that the longer we stay in office, the harder it gets to stay any longer. This is the problem we inherit from having made them children: they need change and variety, and so, because we are here to stay, there is a problem. The voters grow tired of us, and thus incumbency after a while almost insures that our opponents will be able to mount a significant challenge against our political future. The only way to avoid this problem is somehow to dispense with the voter or the vote. Until we figure that one out, we have to meet the challenge of our opposition. Democracy is the larger problem here, but that is an issue for another time, for we now have a job to do. After all, we are the people's choice—for now anyway.

Lest you think the tone of this letter too dour, given the problems with voters, the rest of the letter will simply serve to remind you of the tremendous advantages we have over our opponents when we oppose them at election time.

We prey upon the weaknesses of voters, and because the vices of people almost always exceed their virtues, we have chosen the stronger suite, which is to say their weaknesses. We therefore use and exploit envy, fear, selfishness, and self-pity for our political gain. Of course there are other human vices, but these are our strongest because they are the ones to which people are most prone and therefore exceedingly susceptible. They are also vices capable of infinite manipulation by us. Our trick is to present policies to the voter which will accommodate these weaknesses, at least in part, with of course a careful wording which will make the policies look not only just and fair, but of course also respectful of equality. In truth, most of our policies will serve opposite purposes.

We do not have to have all the votes, so we figure on losing certain blocs of voters, but we have to know who these votes represent, so that we know at all times the voting habits of the company we keep: thus, whom we can afford to offend and when we need to genuflect. Added to this is the fact that we never write off any block of voters, until there is the nearly certain belief that to do so will bring in a larger block of voters. This is why, for example, we can assail the rich relentlessly. As a group they are very small, and the amount of loathing directed toward this small group of voters by other voters is sufficiently huge to show that by castigating the smaller group we can garner the votes of the larger group. This calculation is merely arithmetical, but also beautifully illuminating.

That being said, and as you can see, we divide and conquer; we do not, therefore, unite but fragment. The trick is simply to have the largest fragments when the voters go to vote. We of course continue to talk about unity. We talk about unity when it is to our advantage and its opposite when that is to our advantage. With a ratcheting up of your political skills you will be able to do both in the same political speech—in fact, in the same sentence.

Finally, keep your voters happy, and by the fact that you won your election, you will be keeping the majority of voters happy. The best way to do this is to present a few presents to them—legislation long in waiting will do—within your first days in office. Lest their enthusiasm for you dim after the last present is given on that occasion, simply remind them that in the very near future there will be many more where those came from.

Dear Purefoy,

No, we have no other gods except ourselves, so we do on occasion allow a substitute for numerous reasons. Sometimes we just need a vacation. It is not without warrant that even superstitious cultures such as ours imagine their god needful of rest at least once a week. We are not superstitious, but we need rest too. We get tired also of having to fulfill the default role of god after a while, even though most of our voters don't yet think of us as such, so we have to permit belief in something else on occasion, however ridiculous. A good crisis or two are usually sufficient to send people running to their gods—Us in time we hope, whether the ignorant voters suspect we are standing in waiting or not.

Our dearest mother, Mother Earth, is our current god, adored by many of our people, such as She is. There is, of course, not just implicit danger from courting this notion, but real peril, as some of our own crawl back to religion with a more ridiculous notion than that our religious fathers abandoned decades ago. In other words, within our own camp there are religious cravings that must be watched and contained, until that craving turns toward respecting ourselves as the only god the people need. If the current pull and frenzy toward patching our relationship with nature becomes too serious, we could see some of our own claiming that government itself is unnatural. This view could spell disaster for our political intentions, as I have mentioned to you before. So while we tolerate this latest craving for religion, we only tolerate it, but have little sympathy for it. Furthermore, it reflects much ignorance, most of it willful, of our glorious past that dispensed with belief in God.

The current hankerers after religion in our camp forget that our secular predecessors abandoned their culture's god some ages ago and for good reason. They did so when enough cataclysmic events undermined their belief that any god worth his salt would have mercifully constructed his universe without one or the other—humans or evil. If this supposed god had any care at all for the miserable beings having to live in such a world he would have rebuilt this mess he forced people to live in, or at least kept people out of it. He did neither, so our intellectuals after a while decided they would be done with any such god. They would simply accept the world as it was, warts and all—but no god with it. Therefore, we assume the role of the absent god, though we continue to have competitors. Mother Earth is the latest one. As Her head has been raised, the pious among us have lowered their own heads, and with it, their brains.

Our theologians these days are so pampering of our dear Mother that they cannot bear to criticize Her, much like the faith theologians of previous ages until our secular predecessors started to clamor for reason in matters of religion. The current religion has no such discipline such as reason requires. Thus, when She has a tantrum, such as a bit of volcanic activity or a tsunami or a hurricane, these new theologians rack up all the blame to human wretches. Mother is seen as simply expressing her displeasure at our impious activity which wrecks her internal parts, and causes her to convulse. I will of course admit that this ridiculous notion provides us with gargantuan amounts of political propaganda, but it is nevertheless preposterous and after a while hard to stomach. I never prayed to the old god; I am not going to start praying to a new one.

First of all, when we got rid of the old god, we came to the realization at the same time that nature has no moral tentacles and no moral sensibilities. All the religious portends that were thought to be the "message" of comets and volcanic activity and the like crashed to earth when our secular saviors explained them without the ignorance that had advanced the religious "message" hypothesis about the workings of nature. In other words, there is nothing more to nature than how nature blindly works. Nature manifests no secret plans, or for that matter, any plan at all. The most we can say, and even this is a gigantic amount of anthropomorphism, is that nature works for herself with no thought for us, for nature has nothing that remotely resembles "thoughts." In other words, nature does what nature does, with no thought for anything. Even the term "Nature" is meaningless, because it suggests an overarching planning facility in charge of the whole course of the workings of our world. However, Nature is as blind as a bat and the way she operates is without any moral deliberation whatsoever. In fact, there is no deliberation. Morals are our own human invention: they do not belong to Her. This Mother Nature stuff is therefore dangerous because it suggests that there is something of a relationship between Her and us. There is nothing of the sort. We are it. There is nothing else.

The true picture of Nature therefore leaves us with nothing to bow before, but only with an indifferent and recalcitrant and resisting enemy of which we should be wary, for she shall take our life tomorrow, or next year, or the next decade with bacteria or viruses or floods or droughts or earthquakes. If you manage to avoid these, your own internals shall claim your life, with stopping hearts and the like. She wills even mutations to get around our antibiotics when we resist Her. Her quiver of the vehicles of Her wrath, as plentiful as Her actions, stand poised to present untold obstacles toward our well-being. None of this activity, however, has anything to do with us. Her actions are not even remotely "personal." There is no intention or anything of the sort on Her part. She cares nothing for us because She has nothing with which to evoke such feelings. She has no conscience because She has neither mind nor morals. She does what She does for the simple reason that She does it; our genuflecting and ignorant theologians nevertheless bow before Her in mindless reverence. It would be laughable if it were not so stupid—and dangerous.

Our pious theologians, moreover, are as stupid as the men of old who bowed and sacrificed in front of a stone or block of wood. Today, however, our pious theologians are imagining that Mother is talking through her gesticulating actions, which for the most part evidence her anger toward the trespassers who walk and plow and build highways and malls and factories across her face and cloud her skies with suet and smog and the like. And just like the pious followers of the old god, these new earth theologians see Mother's activity as not to be questioned. The old problem of evil therefore is not entertained, because it would signal the death of yet another aspiring god. That is, what killed the old god will not be allowed to kill the new god, and the problem will not even be raised so as to preserve the belief in Her as our dearest Mother. Thus, the new theologians can only avoid this same deadly thing happening to their benevolent Mother by ignoring the actions of dearest deity Mother Earth. The truth of the matter is that she is a beast as ready to devour us as to help us. The fact of the matter is that there is no Mother Earth anymore than there was a Father God.

Dear Purefoy,

Yes, your opponent is no longer your immediate obstacle. The needs of your voters are your concern. Remember the voters you have to keep; your opponent you destroyed, politically. Of course, you defeated your opponent in the present, but she or others like her will return. For the time being, and because you were elected, and not your opponent, you should turn more toward your voters than our frazzled opponents. Fortunately for us our opponents are presently in a free fall and their nightmarish worry is when, if ever, they will come out of their plummet. Defeat has disgraced them. If you respond to your voters appropriately, our political opponents may never witness an end to their punitive descent, and thus their final demise may be in the near future. Thus, by keeping your voters satiated and happy, we will decisively defeat your future opponents even before their names are known. Keeping your voters happy works more ill for your opponent than if you attack him. You can politically kill your opponent by being kind to your voter. This is why I said to you toward the end of your campaign that a successful campaign should be measured by how little you speak about your opponent. Indeed, in a perfect campaign, you would never need to even mention him at all.

The anxiety of our voters—but before that—here I must respond to your question. Despite the opportunities before us, we take nothing for granted. Thus, the election is really never over, and it is your naïve mistake to think there is a time—you imagine it as now, after your election—when you are not running for office. You are always running for office. This means that your campaign never comes to an end, even after you are elected or reelected. Of course, you do not talk that way in the presence of your constituents, but the point is you always position yourself in such a way that all that you do and say is construed and calculated for your next bid for election. That is simply another element of our reigning political philosophy that all things are political. We have not a single bone of the statesman in us; we are politicians.

The country is now understandably anxious and nervous. As I said to you prior to your election, this state of affairs presents us with gigantic opportunities, but handled unwisely, such financial tremors could prove detrimental for us if a wrong course of action or response is offered. Caution must always be exercised.

The fact of the matter is that none of us have a sliver of certitude about how to calm our gyrating and sinking economy. We know how to calm the voters, but calming the economy is another matter. We of course have our usual idea of pumping money into an economy rapidly losing money, but taking from ourselves to pay ourselves has its limitations. This is not taking from Peter to pay Paul, but Peter taking from Peter to pay Peter and Paul taking from Paul to pay Paul. That point aside, what the voter must see in us is a picture of calm serenity when the waters are choppy. Furthermore, if the ship of state is being tossed around ferociously, we must remain steadfast in our poised attention on the obstacles our voters face. Our response is nevertheless all window dressing, though not precisely intended for deception, but for calming our voters. But there is more.

An appearance of calmness in no way undermines my earlier advice of some weeks ago, when the first real perceptions of what was to come became evident to us. That is, we get political traction when the ground is shaking, and if it is not shaking we try to convince our voters that it is. We do the reverse for the reverse situation. That is, when the ground is shaking, we tell our voters not to worry because they have us, and in us they have solidity. So in the one case we create fear; in the other we take it away. The middle ground of transition between the two we play to whichever is of most political benefit to us at the moment.

Of course we are for financial bailouts of various sorts. In fact, there is hardly one that we could imagine being against: school bailouts, union bailouts, kindergarten bailouts, spa bailouts, lodge bailouts, bar bailouts, and of course, as needed—business bailouts. Our reasoning, which I have conveyed to you many times, is simple. The money makers of our country we loathe, because we purport to loathe money while we love people. We nevertheless are in the business of propagating a political ideology predicated on the belief that people have a right to money. It is our most basic belief; therefore, our hatred of money does not cause us to spurn money, but to take it as we wish in our belief that people without it, or without enough of it, have a right to it or to more of it. We aim therefore to eradicate the class of have-nots. We have as our goal a classless society. In effect, we hate the money others have, while we love the money that we have. This constitutes, therefore, our love/hate relationship with money. We loathe it when someone else has what we could have. To take it without benefit of law would be stealing; to take it under the cover of law is "Social Justice." The vast majority of voters love us for it, because they always want more and never less.

All this is to say that bailouts are necessary, because the money providers of our mammoth government of everything for everybody must not be too severely choked; this is because they produce the money we take and redistribute. So again, and now and forever, we can have our cake and eat it too. That is, we can chastise the greed of our money-makers while filling our buckets with the product of their work. So we give the appearance of being prepared to shut them down because of their greed, but when they appear to be gasping for their last breath, we "rescue" them from their destruction.

Thus, to keep our voters happy, they must be kept in money. To keep them in money, the money producers must be making money, so we can milk them of it. Where they are not making money, we pump money into them, so they can resume making money. When your voter sees this taking place, he will tend to think this is not only an adequate response, but a humane and responsible one.

There is also a long term benefit to our current financial crisis and what we are doing about it. It simply allows our politicians in government to start to assume greater power over these renegade market forces—the vaunted but enslaving "free" market. For example, we may, if our insiders are savvy enough to accomplish it, force the auto manufactures to make only the kind of automobiles we the government want for the people. This puts us in charge of the producers and the people.

Dear Purefoy,

Yes, there is a work of rehabilitation going on with the new regime at it comes to power. That rehabilitation concerns our standing in the world. This change will be difficult, simply because we are at such a low position in the estimation of the world at large. Nevertheless, we will see our stature raised from a trough to a trophy. Our new comrade—we loathe the militaristic designation commander-in-chief—will show the world that we have no aggressive tendencies toward any nation of the world, no matter who or how many belligerents line up against us. As I told you some time ago, war is a thing of the past. The future will know nothing of it, and we will justly claim credit for this latest piece of human evolution. In time our grandchildren, when they study history, will ask us, "What was the thing called 'war?'" We will resolve our conflicts in this age with reason, not weapons. Once our "enemies" understand that, they will throw their own weapons down, and we will realize to our utter dismay and dissatisfaction, that they only had their weapons in position because they saw ours. We have thus led with bad example before now; now and in the future we shall lead with good example. Once our present "enemies" see we intend no harm toward them, they will no longer desire to harm us. The mammoth amount of revenue we can garner from dissolving our military will be gigantic. Every tank or weapon that is built is a school or community center or spa not built. The previous machinery of war will be recycled and rebuilt for peace. Military museums will start to take on the aura of museums about the distant past. Indeed, the ages of war in time will become as distant as the age of the dinosaurs.

I see that you still have not fully grasped the political value of using the terms "community," or "sense of community," or "building community." This is a huge mistake, for by such notions we commend ourselves to our voters. Even more importantly, by all such words we muffle any antagonist who opposes our principles. To oppose "community" is to exhibit a motive of selfishness which we justly criticize as being indifferent or hostile to "community." The word "private" for such reasons always provokes an air of suspicion to us. It connotes fences and borders. As a member of the "community," by contrast, one exhibits selflessness. You see, to be for "community" is to be for the "common good," not the uncommon good or the individual private good. The latter, in fact, are not good, but the opposite. In a word, getting our voters to affectionately gravitate toward "community" is simply another step toward socialism, which amounts to much of the same thing. If we build our communities into what we want, one day they will awaken to see that they are socialists without the word. By then, in love with the community they—rather, we—have fashioned, such persons will no longer find themselves averse toward the hallowed word. Like the wars we have ridded them of for the cause of eternal peace, so too they will feel understandable regret that they did not become socialists earlier.

You need to constantly increase the size of "community," until there are virtually no persons that matter to us outside "the community." Remember, as I have often said, we are not for all, but for the most. This in effect means that you have no opponents whom you do not wish to have as opponents. This means too that belligerents who are not part of the "world community," must therefore be brought within it—but of course only the ones we want in our community. This means also that one thing that gives the gangs of community their power is the intimidation they bring to bear upon their enemies. Who are our enemies? Those who do not want to fall into the lock-step movement of "community." And he who commands the largest "community," commands respect of the mob under which the "community" façade establishes itself. Communities are faceless; their leaders give them the face they have. Let the power of this idea sink into your thinking, and then act on it.

You see, we take respected terms and we turn them into terms that we can use to mask well nigh everything. This is the power of our word "community," that we use it to indicate a selfless adherence and respect for others, with the impression given of no thought for the self and its selfish interests. The term as we use it thus conveys the idea of the cohesive element of community, and not the tyrannical power that comes with it. We, however, simply abuse the cohesion for the tyranny which cohesion offers to muffle dissidents. Furthermore, in "community" as we would have it, there is the goal of equality, so we can exert our leverage against any differences amongst people unfavorable to our political gain. Remember, our ultimate goal is everything for everybody, with no distinctions among any. Remember too that our "any" and "all" language is a façade for the most.

If this provokes any rebellion, we need not worry, for as long as we have the allegiance of the "community" we will have everything needed to put it down. Thus we aim for the tyranny of the majority against the minority by making sure we are always in command of the majority—or the "community."

Furthermore, we have groomed a "community" which in appearance looks like the oppressed minority of the past, except we have now made it the oppressing majority of the present. This we do of course by making our adults into demanding children, and we are only too willing to meet the demands of "community" in exchange for their vote.

Ponder these things in your heart, but meanwhile, go out and build some "community."

Dear Purefoy,

Yes, you are mingling with the right crowd; "Rolling up your sleeves is getting on your knees" is precisely the sort of harmless religious duty that easily works itself into our politics and in time forgets about and even spurns religion. You are clearly moving in the correct religious circles if the congregation you speak of has such a religious posture. As I have indicated to you many times, this country is soaked in religious piety, but we are slowly and effectively secularizing the "sacred." The group you speak of, it sounds like, are already halfway there. Remember, we are materialists, not spiritualists; therefore we are in the business of conversion, though not to religion. Unless we can make religious piety work for us, we have no use for it. If you have to court the spiritualists because you are having trouble from some of them, the first thing to do is to assess their numbers. If they are negligible, they are too few voters to concern yourself with, and as long as their voices do not get too loud, they do not constitute an object of real concern. If larger blocks of voters start to tag along as your ever present critic, then you have something to be concerned about. This almost never happens, because the country is sliding toward secularism, and the call to reverse it, to call for "revival," is anachronistic to most all our citizens. One might as well call for the earth to be flat again.

So, we still tote religion along with us, but we never let the wrong religion get too close to us. In times of crisis more of our constituents will call for their god to get close to them and their shaking world, but when you show them government can do more for them than their god ever did, then they will forsake god for you. One does not really have to tell them that, because you can show them.

Since we are drawing so close to our beloved socialism these days, it is perhaps time to consider the next stage of our political planning: socialism without votes. This must be undertaken incrementally, and might start by annulling the current term limits on some of our political offices. After that, it might take the form of arguing that because the polling numbers of an office holder are so astronomically high, it would be a waste of money to run a needless election to confirm what the voters want when they have already confirmed it through polling. You can of course see the huge potential of moving away from the ballot box. The great thing about democracy is that the will of the people can bring about well nigh anything. They can even annul democracy if they want to.

Dear Purefoy,

"Recounts" are never a liability for us, only assured assets; they are truly opportunities awaiting response from us. We simply manufacture the needed votes for our candidate until we have enough to make that candidate the winner. Then we "find" these ballots. Of course there will be objections from our opponents, because there always are—but we simply persist with our principle of "counting all the votes." We utter this mantra *ad infinitum*, and few dare to ask where the votes came from that we are counting. This insistence on counting all the votes immediately puts our opponent at a grave disadvantage in the public eye, for it looks as if he is trying to obstruct the very thing we are intent to ensure. Meanwhile, we continue to procure and, where necessary, produce ballot after ballot until our candidate has more ballots in his favor than the opponent. Any protest against our efforts will be met with the principled axiom that we simply wanted all the votes counted. We include even the ones we manufacture. Remember, we do not work for nothing, but for getting elected. We expect and get rewards for our efforts.

Nevertheless, to detour scrutiny away from ourselves and onto safer terrain, we talk about the voters rather than our vote finders and counters. This of course is one more time and occasion to get mileage out of the "disenfranchised" voter, for we will contend that bullies are using intimidation and clubs to keep the "wrong" kind of voter away from the voting booth. Of course, this "disenfranchised" voter is the voter who favors us and our candidates. All other things aside, our opponent knows that these voters are our voters and that the disenfranchised voting bloc belongs to us and not to him.

The disenfranchised voter, our voter, has trouble getting himself to the voting booth. He is not blocked from access to the booth by our opponents; he is his own block. That does not matter, however, for we accommodate his disability in getting him to the voting place. His trouble is our opportunity. This in itself makes him a tremendous resource for us. Therefore we get him to the place, and better, lots like him. We go into every alley and side street and back street and ravine and gorge and cavern and tavern to pull out these voters, because their votes will overwhelmingly vote for us. Our opponent knows this, but he is hard pressed to do much about it, because he knows these voters are simply exercising their lawful right to vote. And all votes are equal; the winner is the winner by having more votes, not better votes. Quantity is all that matters when it comes to voting; quality is irrelevant. The vote of an idiot is equivalent to the vote of the intellectual.

Thus, we can ensure and ultimately guarantee an election outcome by hauling out masses of the ignorant vote, after this previously non-voting but very sizeable number has been coaxed by us to vote for us. By extending this sort of push for gang voting as a way of ensuring votes for victory, in time we will be capable of producing enough voters like these to win virtually any and every election. Meanwhile, these same voters—who have hardly any investment in the country which produces their entitlements—run the country with their votes. These "powerless" or the "disenfranchised," whichever term you prefer, now can have ultimate power because we have empowered them to have power by voting for us. They will thus become the new and very large luxury class, who pay virtually nothing in exchange for most everything. The disenfranchised will have the power to run the country. The servant has become the master, and the old master is now slaving for his prior servant while he, the old master, is accordingly abused as the former servant was. A beautiful turn of history—and all due to us!!

You may think this scenario far into the future, but it is closer than you think. Just look at the burgeoning number of voters these days that pay hardly a cent in taxes due to our lovingly conceived progressive tax code, complete with credits of a casino sort, except they are assured. Though we recruit more voters from this group of people each day, we still have seen only the tip of the iceberg. Those voters who don't cast a vote—who exist as the other half of the public that could vote—will belong to us, and dangling enough promised money and goodies in front of them to persuade them to vote for us will not be difficult. It will not require excessive toil. They are an untapped and gigantic resource for us. When we tap a sufficient number of them, we will hardly need to bother with a campaign anymore. And when a campaign becomes unnecessary, an election will become unnecessary. The "will of the people" will stoutly will that we have power for all time. They, for their part, can have uninterrupted time in their sand box, knowing that we will always supply them with sand.

LaVergne, TN USA
16 February 2010
173274LV00004B/4/P

9 781600 474088